Praise for Mikaela Martinez and
Big Projects for Little Learners

"Today's teachers and parents are inundated with information. They don't need more advice—they need tools they can actually implement. And not just any tools—ones that are meaningful, child-centered, and that kids will enjoy. This book does the heavy lifting, making project-based learning approachable, doable, and genuinely joyful."

—Elizabeth Mundt,
Educator and Creator of @thekidlitmama

"*Big Projects for Little Learners* makes project-based learning feel so doable and tangible for early childhood educators including myself. Mikaela helps you feel empowered to do these types of projects with your students, giving you a detailed road map for multiple individual projects, while also validating your experience as a teacher who wants to respect the interests and voice of your students."

—Holly Hodges,
Founder of Research and Play LLC

"Mikaela has thoughtfully created an easy-to-follow guide for all teachers to use as a resource for not only the littlest of learners but for ALL learners. As a teacher myself, I find benefit in the joyful, authentic, and student-centered approach Mikaela has laid out in her lessons as a PBL expert."

—Jana Durbin,
1st, 2nd, and 3rd grade advisor at Jeffco Open and PEBC Lab Host

"Drawing on years of hands-on experience designing Project-Based Learning in both traditional and innovative learning settings, Mikaela Martinez offers educators a clear road map to PBL infused with practical tools, heartfelt stories, and a deep understanding of how young children learn best. This essential guide includes 52 thoughtfully crafted and classroom-tested units that prove even the youngest learners can engage in powerful, real-world work."

—Maya Lê,
Creator of MaiStoryBook

BIG PROJECTS FOR LITTLE LEARNERS

BIG PROJECTS FOR LITTLE LEARNERS

A PBL GUIDE FOR THE HOME AND CLASSROOM

Mikaela Martinez

JB JOSSEY-BASS™
A Wiley Brand

Library of Congress Cataloging-in-Publication Data

Names: Martinez, Mikaela author
Title: Big projects for little learners : a PBL guide for the home and
  classroom / Mikaela Martinez.
Description: Hoboken, New Jersey : John Wiley & Sons, Inc, [2026] |
  Includes index.
Identifiers: LCCN 2025027945 (print) | LCCN 2025027946 (ebook) | ISBN
  9781394319022 paperback | ISBN 9781394319046 adobe pdf | ISBN
  9781394319039 epub
Subjects: LCSH: Project method in teaching | Early childhood
  education–Activity programs
Classification: LCC LB1139.35.P8 M37 2026 (print) | LCC LB1139.35.P8
  (ebook)
LC record available at https://lccn.loc.gov/2025027945
LC ebook record available at https://lccn.loc.gov/2025027946

Cover Illustrations & Design: Paul McCarthy

SKY10126244_091525

This book is dedicated to the learners. To every child who will be impacted by one of the units in this book, you are the teachers of our future. Never stop asking questions.

Contents

Contents

Preface

I had been teaching for a few years when I first stumbled upon Project-Based Learning (PBL) though I didn't know that's what it was called yet. I was in my fourth-grade classroom, planning out these big, intricate units that my teammates lovingly teased me about. "You have way too much time on your hands," they'd say, as I excitedly sketched out plans for classroom book review directories, student-run artifact museums, and Oregon Trail diary projects. But the truth is, that's just how I saw teaching. It's how I loved to learn as a kid, and it's how I wanted my students to experience learning, too.

Looking back now, I can pinpoint where that love started. In third grade, my teacher, Mrs. Hiebert, led us through a year-long study of the world. At the end of the year, we each had this massive D-ring binder filled with everything we'd learned: our maps, our reports, our drawings, our notes. I still have that binder, and when I flip through it now, it's so clear that she was a PBL teacher, even if she didn't call it that. She didn't just teach us content; she created *experiences* that brought learning to life, and I carried that inspiration with me into my own classroom.

Fast forward to my third year of teaching: we were doing a school-wide book study on writing instruction. I was the last to pick a book, so I grabbed *Inside Information* by Nell K. Duke. It was technically for K-2 teachers, definitely not what I was teaching at the time, but I dove in anyway. And let me tell you, it was like someone had flipped on all the lights in my brain. There it was, spelled out for me: *Project-Based Learning.* Everything she described—students learning by engaging in meaningful, real-world work—was exactly what I'd been doing. I finally had a name for it, and better yet, I knew this style of teaching was impactful, intentional, and so important.

Not long after, I heard that a new elementary school was opening in a nearby district, and it was going to be entirely PBL-focused. I couldn't get there fast enough. I sat down with the principal and said, "I know you don't know me, and I've only taught fourth grade, but give me a kindergarten classroom, and I promise I won't let you down." That was the start of a five-year journey in a K-5 PBL public school, the first of its kind in our state. Those years were a whirlwind of learning and creating: designing projects, writing units, collaborating with colleagues, and experiencing the magic of hands-on, student-driven learning with the youngest learners.

After five years, I took a leap of faith and started *Project Based Primary*®, my own school and curriculum company for preschool and kindergarten-aged learners. Today, not only do I get to teach young students through PBL, but I also have the privilege of helping other teachers, alternative school leaders, and homeschooling parents bring this powerful teaching approach to life.

Creating your own PBL units can be a daunting task, and that is what this book aims to help you do. When I was first embarking on my teaching journey, making my first unit was no simple task. I scoured books and the internet for units to get me started, and I constantly came up empty handed. Finding quality units for primary learners was like finding a needle in a haystack.

So, I decided to begin writing them myself. Creating units that covered the standards and content I was expected to teach, and units that covered content my students were curious and enthusiastic about. Over the years, I have written 52 complete PBL units. I have had the chance to teach almost all of them in my own classrooms, testing out and altering them as needed to best fit the needs of my learners. And now I am excited to share them all with you!

Introduction

As you journey through this book, think of it as your personal PBL manual. This book opens with an overview of PBL, what it is, what characterizes it, and why it is so impactful for students. It covers each one of the seven key elements of PBL: Challenging Problem or Question, Sustained Inquiry, Authenticity, Student Voice and Choice, Reflection, Critique and Revision, and Public Product. Once you have read through Chapter 1, you will have a solid knowledge and foundation about the WHAT and WHY of PBL. You can reference this chapter throughout your teaching and learning to anchor your understanding of the different elements of a unit, and when developing your own units.

As you move into Chapters 2 through 6, you will get to put this knowledge into practice. Throughout the chapters, I outline 52 unique PBL units. Each unit provides a driving question, a public product, a launch event, three completely fleshed out modules including a mini driving question for each. Within each module are all the lessons and activities you will want to cover to guide your learners through the unit. These lessons include inviting in experts, going on community expeditions, collaborating with peers, providing critique and feedback, and ample opportunity for student voice and choice. There is also an exhibition event idea that helps you easily provide an authentic audience for students to share their final product.

Throughout the units, I also include ways to alter the unit for homeschooling families, micro schools, alternative learning environments, and smaller groups. These units can be done by anyone with just small changes throughout them to meet your individual needs. They are flexible in nature, so these small changes do not detract from the unit as a whole.

Within the units are also references to specific learning resources and materials that I have created for my students to accompany these units. If you scan the QR code in the appendix of this book, you will be directed to the printable learning materials that can pair with your teaching and student learning.

Once you have tried out a few of the units I have authored, you are also ready to give creating your own units a try! The final section of this book walks you step-by-step through my exact planning process. I guide you through the backward planning method that I use every time I am creating a new unit. It ensures you have incorporated all of the seven key elements, integrated your teaching and learning standards, and developed lessons and experiences that are developmentally appropriate and engaging to your learners. I have also included all of the planning and organizational templates I have created and use to plan every element of my units so that you can plan alongside me as you read!

01 What Is Project-Based Learning?

Project-Based Learning, or PBL, is a way of teaching where even our youngest learners, preschoolers, and kindergarteners get to learn by *doing*. Instead of sitting at tables completing worksheets or memorizing facts, kids work on meaningful projects that connect to the real world, spark their curiosity, and make learning hands-on. These projects aren't just about cutting, gluing, and crafting for fun (although there's plenty of that in the process). PBL gives learners a chance to ask big questions, solve real problems, and share their discoveries with others.

For example, imagine a class of preschoolers noticing that birds visit the playground every day. Their teacher sparks a project by asking, "How can we take care of the birds who visit our playground?" The kids might explore what birds eat by reading picture books, watching videos, and observing birds outside. They could design and build bird feeders using recycled materials, test out different spots to see where birds visit the most, and even document the types of birds they see in a "Bird Journal."

At the end of the project, the kids could invite parents or other classes to see their feeders and share what they've learned about caring for birds. Along the way, they're learning about science (habitats, animals, and weather), math (measuring and counting materials), and literacy (writing signs, reading stories, and sharing their observations). And because it's tied to something *real*, helping birds they see every day, they're naturally excited and invested.

This chapter will walk you through the concept of PBL, and what makes it work so well in the classroom (or for homeschooling). But before I dig into *what* Project-Based Learning is, let's talk about what it isn't.

PBL Is Not a Curriculum

PBL isn't a curriculum, it's a teaching method, a delivery system for all the skills and standards we need to teach. It's not about "fun projects" that happen at the end of a unit, like making sugar cube pyramids or dioramas of castles. Those are *projects*, but they're not *Project-Based Learning*. PBL is different. It's a method where students become active participants in their learning. They tackle real-world problems, research meaningful questions, work together as a team, and share their work beyond the four walls of the classroom. It's rigorous. It's messy. It's full of inquiry, discovery, and a lot of hard work, for both students and teachers. And the best part? The learning sticks because students care deeply about the work they're doing.

What I love most about the PBL community is that it's built on collaboration, not competition. Teachers swap ideas, ask for feedback, share resources, and cheer each other on. We're all in it for the same reason: to create meaningful learning experiences for students that help them think critically, solve problems creatively, and grow into confident, capable humans.

For me, PBL is the most powerful and purposeful way to teach. It's what keeps me excited to walk into the classroom every single day, and it's why I'm so passionate about sharing it with others. So, if you're ready to reimagine what teaching and learning can look like, let's dive in!

Curiosity Is the Key

The key to PBL in early childhood classrooms is that it's driven by kids' natural curiosity and questions. For instance, if a child asks, "Where does our food come from?" that could lead to a project about gardening. The class might plant seeds, track their growth, and learn about what plants need to thrive. They could build a simple garden box, take care of the plants, and eventually harvest vegetables to taste or share with families. This kind of project builds science skills (learning about plants and life cycles), math skills (counting seeds, measuring soil or water), and language skills (documenting growth through drawings and words). Plus, it connects kids to their world in a real, meaningful way.

But here's what makes PBL different from "just doing projects" or one-off activities: It's about the process, not just the product. If a group of kindergarteners builds a cardboard bridge as part of a project on transportation, it's not about whether the bridge looks perfect. It's about the conversations they had while building, the teamwork they practiced when deciding how to put it together, and the problem-solving they did when it collapsed, and they had to try again. When they test toy cars on it and shout, *"It works!"* they're not just learning about bridges, they're learning to persevere, experiment, and think like engineers.

Students work collaboratively to test their structures and add design details.

In PBL, kids aren't passive learners. They're active participants, driven by their curiosity, creativity, and need to explore the world around them. The work is real and meaningful.

With PBL, kids don't just color pictures to learn how an animal looks. Instead, they might create habitats for toy animals using boxes, fabric, and blocks. When kindergarteners learn about weather, they don't just memorize seasons; instead, they might design "weather stations" to observe rain, wind, and temperature outside. These projects make learning stick because the kids are *experiencing* it, not just hearing about it.

And perhaps most importantly, PBL builds the foundational skills that kids need for a lifetime of learning. It encourages them to ask questions, think critically, collaborate with their peers, and share their ideas with confidence. They learn that their ideas matter, their work has purpose, and they are capable of solving problems, even at three, four, five, or six years old. When you see a group of preschoolers proudly showing off the bug hotels they built or hear a kindergartener explaining how they planted a garden, you realize that this is more than just "cute projects." This is real, meaningful learning that kids will carry with them long after they leave your classroom.

The Benefits of Project-Based Learning

The benefits of PBL in education are hard to overstate; it's the kind of teaching and learning that doesn't just check off standards but actually makes a lasting impact. PBL makes learning meaningful, engaging, and real, and the results back it up. When kids are actively involved in their own learning, asking questions, solving problems, and creating something they care about, they grow in ways that traditional methods just can't replicate.

Let's start with engagement because anyone who's spent time with kids knows that engagement is half the battle. Research shows that PBL leads to higher levels of student engagement because kids are *invested* in the work they're doing. A study from the Buck Institute for Education (now PBLWorks) found that "92% of teachers reported an increase in student engagement when they implemented PBL." And this makes sense, right? When learning is hands-on, relevant, and connected to real life, kids are excited to show up. They're not just completing tasks to please the teacher, they're exploring big questions, working on projects they care about, and sharing their work with others.

I've seen this firsthand. During a kindergarten project focused on "How do different animals survive and thrive?" students decided they needed to learn all they could about their favorite animals and share it with others. They were obsessed with the National Geographic readers about animals, the kind with the yellow borders, and they wanted to write their very own versions of those books. The kids deep dove into animals in research teams, created 3D models of the animals, designed and painted murals that depicted their habitats, and wrote their very own nonfiction animal books, complete with the yellow border. The kids didn't just learn about animals; they opened an entire school zoo. They gave tours to the whole school, members of the school board and district office administrators came, and these five- and six-year-olds were confidently and proudly teaching everyone about the animals and reading their books to them. And they were *excited* to do it!

One little girl told me, "I was so nervous to give a zoo tour, but I am so proud I did it. I am ready to do it again." That excitement and ownership? That's the magic of PBL. And this is one of my favorite parts of this way of teaching: It nurtures kids' confidence. When students see that their ideas matter, when they solve a problem or create something that makes a real difference, their confidence soars. The research backs this up, too. PBL helps students develop what's known as "self-efficacy," the belief that they can tackle challenges and accomplish goals. A 2021 study published in the *Journal of Educational Psychology* found that ". . .students who participated in PBL demonstrated stronger problem-solving abilities and higher levels of confidence in their learning." These are kids who aren't afraid to try, fail, and try again, because they've experienced the process of solving problems firsthand.

But the benefits of PBL go beyond engagement and building resilient students; PBL also improves academic outcomes.

In a 2016 study published in the *Interdisciplinary Journal of Problem-Based Learning*, researchers found that ". . .students in PBL classrooms performed better on assessments of content knowledge compared to their peers in traditional classrooms." Another study, funded by Lucas Education Research and conducted by Stanford University, showed that ". . .elementary students who learned science through PBL achieved significantly higher test scores than those taught using traditional methods."

Students plant the seeds in their garden.

Why? Because when students learn by doing, when they *experience* the content and see its relevance, they retain it. They aren't just memorizing for a test; they're building understanding that lasts. And it's not just content knowledge; PBL strengthens essential skills that kids need for the future, too. In a world where information is everywhere, success depends on skills like critical thinking, collaboration, and problem-solving. According to the World Economic Forum, ". . .by 2030, 85% of the jobs that will exist haven't even been invented yet." That's a sobering thought, but it's an exciting one because PBL prepares kids for exactly that kind of future. It teaches them how to learn, adapt, and think creatively, no matter what challenges come their way.

Another benefit? PBL helps kids see learning as connected and purposeful. In a traditional classroom, subjects often feel isolated: Math happens during math time, reading happens during reading time, and science gets its own slot. But real life doesn't work like that. When kindergarteners build a classroom garden, they're counting seeds and measuring soil (math), learning about plants and weather (science), reading about gardening (literacy), and writing labels for their plants (writing). It all connects. PBL mirrors the way the world works, and it helps kids see learning as something meaningful and integrated.

Finally, PBL builds a classroom culture that's collaborative, curious, and full of joy. Kids learn to work together, share ideas, and celebrate each other's successes. They learn that mistakes aren't something to fear, they're part of learning. They ask questions and see themselves as capable thinkers who can figure things out. And that, to me, is the biggest benefit of all: Project-Based Learning helps kids love learning. It taps into their natural curiosity and creativity, and it shows them that learning is something they *do*, not something that's done *to* them.

In the end, Project-Based Learning doesn't just prepare kids for tests, it prepares them for life. It builds thinkers, problem-solvers, and creators. It helps kids see that they can make a difference, even at three to six years old. And when you see a group of little learners proudly sharing their project work, whether it's a bird feeder, a trash-cleanup plan, or a life-size human body diagram, you realize that these aren't just "cute activities." This is the kind of learning that matters. The kind of learning that lasts.

The Key Elements of PBL

When you are designing or implementing a PBL unit there are going to be key elements that are interwoven throughout the unit. These elements are what sets a PBL unit apart from your average class project or thematic study.

The key elements include:

- Challenging Problem or Question
- Sustained Inquiry
- Authenticity
- Student Voice and Choice
- Critique and Revision
- Public Product and Presentation
- Reflection

PBL is most effective when thoughtfully designed around these seven key elements that engage students, promote inquiry, and lead to meaningful learning experiences. In this section, we will explore each of these seven elements of a high-quality PBL unit, breaking down each component with detailed explanations and real-world examples. From crafting a compelling driving question to fostering student voice and choice, each element plays a crucial role in shaping an engaging and rigorous learning experience.

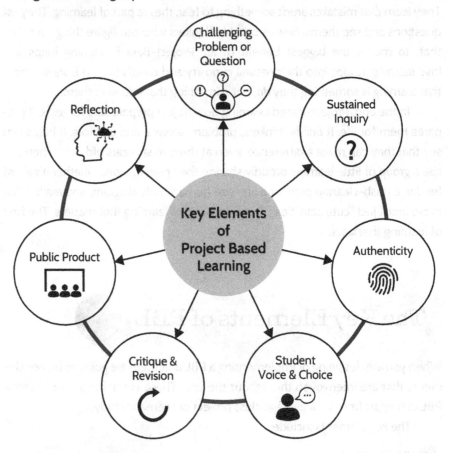

The key elements of PBL.

Challenging Problem or Question

The *Driving Question* is the heartbeat of your Project-Based Learning (PBL) unit. It's the question that keeps you and your learners grounded, the one you return to again and again as the project unfolds. It guides the research, the hands-on work, and the thinking, all while being flexible enough to evolve as kids dig deeper, ask new questions, and revise their ideas along the way.

Now, I'll let you in on a little secret: Coming up with a good Driving Question is often the hardest part of planning a PBL unit. In fact, when I'm planning, I often save it for last. That might sound backward, but backward planning is actually a key part of designing a strong unit. So, if you're feeling stuck, don't let it stop you from diving in. Instead, start by thinking about the big picture:

- What are the learning goals for your students?
- What academic skills or standards do you want them to achieve?
- What kind of real-world problems or outcomes might they explore or create?

Once you've outlined the learning journey and possible project outcomes, you'll be able to craft a thoughtful and meaningful Driving Question that ties it all together.

So, what is a Driving Question? Simply put, it's a question that poses a problem, challenge, or big idea to the learners, one that sparks curiosity, inspires action, and connects their work to the real world. Maybe it's something that hits close to home, like a question about their school or community. Maybe it's something bigger, like helping animals or solving an environmental problem. No matter what it is, the Driving Question gives kids a reason to dig in, ask questions, research, create, and problem-solve, all while understanding that their work *matters*.

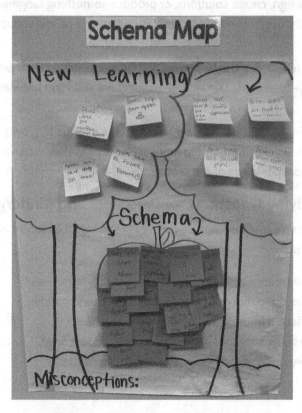

Schema Maps help students hold their thinking surrounding their Driving Question.

What Makes a Great Driving Question?

A great Driving Question serves as the foundation of any Project-Based Learning experience, guiding students through exploration, critical thinking, and real-world application. It's not just a question to answer but a tool to spark curiosity and shape meaningful learning. To craft a truly effective Driving Question, consider these key six characteristics:

1. **Open-Ended:** The question shouldn't have a simple yes or no answer. Instead, it should encourage kids to investigate, explore possibilities, and think critically.
2. **Real-World Connection:** A strong Driving Question connects to something real, an issue, problem, or scenario kids can relate to. This connection gives the project meaning and shows kids why their learning is important.
3. **Cross-Curricular:** The best Driving Questions allow for learning across subjects. A single project might touch on science, math, literacy, art, and even social-emotional skills all at once.
4. **Action-Oriented:** A good question inspires action. It motivates kids to research, design, create solutions, or produce something tangible whether that's a birdhouse, a community clean-up plan, or a peaceful butterfly garden.
5. **Aligned with Learning Goals:** The Driving Question should align with your learning objectives, ensuring kids are building the skills and knowledge they need.
6. **Evolving:** Finally, the question should be flexible enough to grow and change as kids learn. It's okay for them to refine their focus as they discover new ideas or uncover deeper layers of the problem.

Sample Driving Questions for Preschool and Kindergarten

Here are some simple yet powerful examples of Driving Questions that are crafted for early learners:

- "How can we create a peaceful garden that attracts butterflies?"
- "What can we do to make our community cleaner and greener?"
- "How do different birds build their homes?"
- "What makes a healthy meal, and how can we prepare one?"
- "What can we do to help our animal friends in the winter?"

Let's take that first one as an example: "How can we create a peaceful garden that attracts butterflies?" At first glance, it's a beautiful, simple question. But look closer, and you'll see that it's full of opportunities for deep, meaningful learning. Kids might study butterflies through books and videos, observe the plants butterflies like, and design their own garden. They might count seeds and measure soil (math), learn about plant life cycles (science), write plant labels (literacy), and create signs to share what they learned with their families (communication and art). And at the end of the project, when they see a butterfly land on a flower they helped plant, they'll understand that their work had a real impact.

That's what a Driving Question does; it gives kids a purpose. It turns learning into something connected, real, and engaging. It's about doing, creating, and discovering. And the best part? The question may start simple, but the journey it inspires is rich, meaningful, and full of possibility.

Sustained Inquiry

Sustained Inquiry, or the idea that kids can keep researching, questioning, and exploring throughout a project, can feel like a huge roadblock for educators when it comes to early childhood classrooms. I get it. At first glance, it's hard to imagine a group of three- to six-year-olds "doing research" in the way we traditionally think of it. They're not independently reading articles or typing search terms into Google. But here's the thing: *They absolutely can research.* Sustained Inquiry is not only *possible* for our youngest learners, but it's also where some of the richest, most magical learning happens. You just have to get a little creative and set up supports that meet them where they are.

In a strong PBL unit, Sustained Inquiry works like a loop. Kids start with questions (sparked by the Driving Question), they gather information, observe, experiment, and make connections. From there, they form new ideas, test out hypotheses, ask even more questions, and dive deeper into research. It's this ongoing process of wondering, exploring, and connecting the dots that makes PBL so engaging, even for early learners.

The Questions I Hear Most

- "How can kids research if they can't read?"
- "How can they research if they can't write?"
- "Where do they even do research, and how do I manage it?"

Providing research trays with texts, images, and specimens allows all learners to access the material at their level.

Exploring Ideas

These are valid questions, and the answers lie in curating research opportunities that are age-appropriate, hands-on, and full of variety. Young children don't need to read full articles or write lengthy notes to be active researchers. What they *do* need are rich, accessible resources and opportunities to ask questions, explore ideas, and make discoveries. Here's how:

1. **Books:** Nonfiction books are a goldmine. Read them aloud, study the photographs, notice the captions, and talk through the information together. Kids can ask questions like, "Why do butterflies like flowers?" and then look for answers as they examine the details in a book.
2. **Video Clips:** Short, kid-friendly documentaries, nature videos, or even animated explainers can bring topics to life. Whether it's watching bees pollinate flowers or learning how recycling works, video is a powerful research tool for visual learners.

3. **Experts:** Invite experts into your classroom: zoologists, chefs, construction workers, vets, gardeners, or the mayor. Whether they come in person or video chat, experts can answer kids' questions and inspire new ones.

4. **Expeditions:** Get out into the real world! Visit a farm, a local pond, a bakery, or a community garden. Kids can see their research in action, observe details, and ask questions on-site.

5. **The Internet (with support):** Use child-friendly websites with teacher guidance, like National Geographic Kids, or search student-generated questions together as a class. Seeing their questions pop up in search results is exciting and meaningful!

6. **Interviews:** Have kids generate questions to ask others: parents, school staff, neighbors, or even peers. You can send questions via email or write them down, and kids can share the answers they learn with the class.

7. **Experiments:** When kids *do* something, they learn. Design simple experiments that let kids test their ideas and see their research in action. For example, "What makes a toy fun to play with?" could lead to designing and testing a brand new toy.

8. **Group Discussions:** Use shared conversations to build on ideas, answer questions, and record learning as a group. Talk about what kids already know (their *schema*) and what they've discovered through inquiry. Write down their thoughts for everyone to see.

9. **Observation and Journaling:** Young children are naturally observant. Encourage them to notice details in the world around them, whether it's the shape of leaves, the sound of birds, or the colors of insects, and record their findings through drawings, notes, or photos.

One of the biggest hang-ups I see is this: People think "research" means being able to read or write at an advanced level. But here's the truth, our youngest learners are also our most curious learners. They love asking questions. They love investigating. And they rise to the occasion when we provide the right tools and scaffolding. Not every PBL unit will use all of these inquiry methods, but combining just two to three of them gives kids plenty of ways to explore, question, and discover.

Students record their new learning as they research.

Favorite Research Tools for Preschool and Kindergarten

Here are six tried-and-true resources I've used to make research accessible and engaging for little learners:

1. **National Geographic Kids:** Nonfiction books, videos, and an easy-to-navigate website full of information.
2. **Zoo Websites:** Many zoos offer live animal cams, videos, and kid-friendly facts about animals and their habitats.
3. **Smithsonian Learning Lab:** A treasure trove of photographs, videos, audio clips, and resources for kids and teachers.
4. **Kid World Citizen:** Articles, maps, book lists, and topic deep dives for everything from cultures to ecosystems.
5. **Newsela:** Articles that can be adjusted to fit different reading levels, making it perfect for young or emerging readers.
6. **Epic Books:** A subscription-based digital library with 40,000+ books that kids can read themselves or listen to as read-alouds.

Using texts at student levels allows for
independent research.

At the end of the day, Sustained Inquiry isn't about kids "looking up answers"
the way adults do. It's about helping them discover that learning is an active, exciting process. When you see a four-year-old observing ants in the grass or a six-
year-old excitedly sharing what a zoologist told them, you realize that young kids
can research, and they're really good at it. All they need are the right tools, a bit of
scaffolding, and the freedom to let their curiosity lead the way.

Authenticity

The key to creating a highly engaging PBL unit, one that naturally reduces classroom management struggles during project work, is authenticity. When I think of
authenticity, I think about the things that light kids up: topics they can't stop talking
about, books they beg to read again and again, the stories I overhear during play,
the questions that come bubbling out when their curiosity takes hold.

Here's where I start: I take a mental (or written) inventory. What are my kids naturally curious about? What have I noticed in their play or conversations? What topics or skills keep popping up again and again? From there, I start asking myself:

- What could I put out on our learning shelves right now to feed that curiosity?
- Is there enough here to design a full-blown unit?
- Can I combine any of these topics or ideas to make a unit even richer?
- Do I have books or materials to support their exploration?

Provide opportunities for learners to have hands-on experiences with the unit topic.

This is the perfect entry point to bring authenticity into your classroom. Maybe you don't have the time or energy to launch into a full PBL unit right away, and that's okay. Maybe for now, it's just adding some themed shelf work or setting out a basket of books on a topic they can't get enough of. That's still honoring their interests. That's still bringing authenticity into their learning. And as you observe what they gravitate toward, you'll start to see which topics might make a perfect first attempt at a Driving Question.

Now, let's clear up a common misconception: Authenticity in PBL is not the same as thematic learning. Thematic learning takes a single topic and ties it into every part of the day, across all subject areas. For example, your students are interested in frogs. So, you have a frog craft station, frog counters for math work, frog books in a book basket, a frog stuffed animal set up at a station for kids to draw their own frog, etc. It's engaging and honoring their interest in frogs, but it is merely a theme rather than a unit that results in answering a question or solving a problem surrounding frogs. PBL is different. Instead, you're crafting a meaningful, research-rich project centered around a specific topic or problem. And within that project, authenticity comes from the connection, the way the work ties to your learners' interests, their lives, and their communities.

In a PBL unit about frogs you may investigate a local pond in your community that you know frogs reside in. Students may notice the people enjoying the pond leave behind their trash, which endangers frogs and makes it an unsafe habitat. Students will dive into a unit researching and exploring the habitat and ecosystem frogs thrive in, learn about their anatomy, their diet, their unique behaviors and attributes, and how humans are threatening their safety and health. Then they might make posters to hang around the pond reminding visitors to throw away their trash to help protect the frogs. They might even petition the city council to add additional trash cans to the area they found the most trash to make it easier for people to dispose of their trash and keep the pond clean. This takes the interest in frogs to the next level. It takes it from "fun and cute preschool classroom" to "I need to be at school tomorrow because we are saving the frogs that live in our pond and I just can't miss out!"

Why Does Authenticity Matter So Much?

When a PBL unit is authentic, the problem posed, or question asked, means something to your learners. It connects to something they care about, something real in their world, whether that's their home, school, or community. An authentic unit doesn't just check off learning standards; it creates a personal connection that makes the work matter to kids. And when kids see that their work has an impact on the real world, their engagement skyrockets.

For example:

- A question like "How can we educate others on how to keep frog habitats safe?" feels real and important because kids notice the frogs at their local pond every time they go there.
- A project like "What can we do to make our classroom more inviting?" feels meaningful because it directly affects their lives.

When the work feels authentic, kids are invested. They want to research, they want to create, and they want to solve the problem in front of them because it matters to them.

Students see the garden they planted in one unit becoming a habitat for the butterflies they released in the following unit.

Building Authenticity in Your Classroom

Here's my advice: Get to know your learners. Pay attention to the things they care about. Watch for trends in their interests, their play, and their questions. If a group of kids spends a week building elaborate block cities, maybe you design a mini unit around "How can we build a stronger bridge for our toy cars?" If they can't stop talking about animals, maybe it's a project like "What can we do to help animals in our neighborhood?" Even a small, simple project that taps into your students' natural curiosity can transform the energy of your classroom. Not only does it keep kids engaged, but it also builds a sense of community. When learners see their interests, ideas, and questions being valued, when they feel like the things they care about are worth studying, it changes everything. They feel seen, they feel heard, and they're eager to dive in and do the work. Authenticity is where PBL comes to life. It's the difference between kids "doing schoolwork" and kids feeling ownership of their learning. The more authentic your unit, the deeper their engagement, and the stronger your classroom culture will be.

Students work collaboratively to make decorations for their exhibition.

Student Voice and Choice

When people first hear the phrase "Student Voice & Choice" in a Project-Based Learning classroom, they often picture students running the show, deciding every detail and directing the entire unit. But that's not quite how it works! In a PBL classroom, the teacher is still very much in charge, crafting meaningful, authentic units that align with learning standards. What makes PBL special is that within this carefully designed framework, we deliberately create space for students to take the lead in ways that matter. Their voices, preferences, and decisions are not just heard but honored.

Here's the heart of it: Student Voice and Choice isn't about chaos or a free-for-all. It's about balance. We, as teachers, are the facilitators of the learning journey, outlining the path and ensuring the destination aligns with learning goals. But along the way, we hand over the reins in key moments, allowing students to make choices about their learning process, their final product, or the way they share their work. These opportunities are where engagement, ownership, and buy-in truly flourish.

When students feel they have a say in their learning, they are more invested in the process. They work harder, collaborate better, and approach challenges with curiosity instead of resistance. Choosing even one or two opportunities for student decision-making in a unit can completely change the energy in your classroom. Kids aren't just completing assignments; instead, they're making decisions, solving problems, and steering their own learning in ways that feel deeply meaningful.

Implementing Student Voice and Choice

Here's how to implement voice and choice:

1. **Unit Topic:** In some cases, you might let students generate ideas about topics they're interested in and then build a unit around those interests. This doesn't mean throwing out standards or curriculum, it means finding where student passions align with what you're teaching and leaning into that overlap.
2. **Research Methods:** Even if the materials are pre-curated to ensure they're appropriate and aligned with learning goals, students can choose *how* they access information. Will they dive into books, listen to audiobooks, watch video clips, observe photographs, or conduct interviews with experts?

Offering these options gives students control over their learning process while still guiding them toward the needed information.

3. **Sub-Topics to Research:** Within a unit, students can often choose which sub-topics to explore. For example, in a project about animals, one student might focus on zebras while another dives into dolphins. They're all contributing to the same big-picture project but tailoring their learning to their own interests.

Within the Zoologist unit, students get to select the animal they research and present on.

4. **Group Size:** The choice of whether to work independently, with a partner, or in a group can be incredibly meaningful to students. Some learners thrive when working alone, while others need the energy and accountability of a group. Whenever possible, offer flexibility in how students collaborate, or don't.

5. **Exhibition:** An exhibition is when students present their learning and public products to an authentic audience. Here, they can have a say in how and with whom they share their work. Will they give a live oral presentation? Pre-record a video? Create a poster? Will they invite parents, peers, community members, or even specialists in the field? Letting students make decisions about how they present their work makes the process personal and exciting.

6. **Final Product:** Allowing students to choose their final product can be a game-changer, especially for reluctant learners. Maybe one student builds a model, another creates a book, and another produces a short video. All are demonstrating their understanding in ways that work for them, and that flexibility can spark creativity and pride in their work.

A Balanced Approach

Not every unit will include all these options; it would be overwhelming for both students and teachers. Instead, choose one or two areas where students can take the lead. Maybe they decide how to present their work, or maybe they choose their sub-topic to research. Small moments of choice go a long way in fostering engagement and authenticity. The beauty of Student Voice & Choice is that it helps learners see themselves as capable decision makers and active participants in their education. It also builds a strong sense of classroom community, where every voice matters and every learner feels valued. The magic happens when students realize they're not just completing assignments, they're creating, exploring, and making meaningful decisions about their own learning journey.

Critique and Revision

Incorporating critique and revision into a Project-Based Learning (PBL) unit can feel like a daunting task, especially in a preschool or kindergarten setting. But don't let the challenge deter you; this process is both possible and incredibly valuable. Critique and revision, the practice of giving and receiving feedback to refine and improve work, is a life-long skill that will serve children well, not just academically but in every facet of life. So, why not start developing it early?

Young learners are more capable than we often give them credit for. With the right scaffolding and tools, they can engage in meaningful critique and make thoughtful revisions to their work. These practices help build essential skills, from listening and questioning to self-reflection and collaboration, all while fostering a growth mindset.

Critique and revision are at the heart of PBL. They teach students to view their work as a process, not a final product, and to value feedback as a tool for growth. Over time, learners strengthen their ability to:

- Improve research and questioning techniques.
- Refine the quality of their creations.
- Present their ideas more effectively.

By starting these practices young, you're equipping students with the tools they'll need to navigate academic and real-world challenges with confidence and resilience.

Students evaluate their work and make needed changes ahead of exhibition.

How Young Students Can Engage in Critique

Here are five developmentally appropriate ways to guide preschool and kindergarten students through the feedback process:

1. **Gallery Walk:** Set up a classroom "gallery" where students display their works-in-progress. Their peers can walk through the space, observe each product, and share feedback. This feedback can be verbal, written as simple notes (for those ready to write), or discussed as a group.

2. **"I Notice, I Wonder"**: This simple yet powerful framework helps young learners provide constructive feedback. During a presentation or display of work, peers can share:

> **"I notice. . ."** observations about what stands out or what's working well.
> **"I wonder. . ."** questions to spark deeper thinking or suggest areas for refinement.

For example, a child might say, "I notice your butterfly has bright colors. I wonder if you could add more details about where it lives."

3. **Peer Compliments**: Dedicate time for students to share positive and specific praise about their peers' work. Teach them to focus on the details: "I like how you used green for the leaves, it makes your tree look real!" This not only boosts confidence but also trains students to observe and articulate what makes work strong.

Pair Share is used for students to review and give feedback on their work with a partner.

4. **Asking Questions:** Flip the feedback process by having the students presenting their work ask questions to their audience. They might prepare three to four targeted questions, such as:

> "What do you think about the colors I chose?"
> "Is there anything I could add to make my story clearer?"

This approach encourages self-reflection and invites peers to provide focused, actionable feedback.

5. **Putting Feedback into Action:** Once students receive feedback, the next step is to help them synthesize that information and decide how to act on it. Not every piece of feedback needs to be implemented; instead, guide them to identify common threads or recurring suggestions. These patterns often point to the most impactful changes they can make.

> For example:

> If multiple peers say they "wonder about" adding more details, students might focus on enriching their work with specifics.
> If the majority compliment a particular element, they might refine and highlight that strength further.

The goal isn't perfection; it's progress. Encourage learners to embrace revision as part of the creative and learning process.

The Power of Early Critique and Revision

When young students engage in critique and revision, they learn to approach feedback with curiosity instead of defensiveness. They develop the ability to evaluate their own work critically and recognize the value of collaboration. Over time, these skills will shape not just better projects but better learners, ones who see challenges as opportunities and feedback as a gift.

Students reevaluate their work and find places to improve their final product.

In the words of Ron Berger, author of *An Ethic of Excellence*, critique helps students understand that "their work is something to be proud of because it represents their best effort after thoughtful reflection and improvement." And isn't that what we want for all learners, no matter how young they are?

Public Product and Presentation

An exciting part of any Project-Based Learning (PBL) unit is the public product, the moment when students showcase their hard work to an authentic audience. It's the culmination of weeks (or even months) of research, inquiry, critique, revision, and collaboration. It's the big "aha!" moment that leaves people astonished, saying, "I can't believe primary students did this!"

What makes the public product so powerful is that it sets PBL apart from other teaching methods. This is when students step beyond the classroom and into the real world, sharing their work with community members, stakeholders, peers, family, or even experts in the field. These real-world connections make their learning feel meaningful and reinforce its significance.

Zoo enclosures were set up by students to provide tours for their guests.

The public product is where everything comes together: where students take pride in their work, demonstrate their learning, and experience the thrill of sharing their ideas. Whether it's a small-scale project or a grand exhibition, it serves as a powerful reminder that their efforts matter beyond the classroom. It's not just about impressing their teacher; it's about making an impact on a wider audience.

So, start where you are. Begin with what feels manageable and build from there. No matter the size or scale, every public product is a celebration of student effort, creativity, and growth, which is something truly worth sharing with the world. But don't mistake it for just the glitz and glam of a final showcase. The public product is more than a polished end result; it's the bridge between the classroom and the real world, connecting what students have learned to why it matters.

Starting with the End in Mind

When I design a PBL unit, I often start at the end: brainstorming potential public products and authentic audiences. This backward planning approach helps me create a meaningful path to the final product. Once I know what students will create and how they'll present it, I can:

- Align learning standards.
- Gather the right resources.
- Plan checkpoints for progress.
- Identify experts to invite or places to visit.
- Write a Driving Question that ties directly to the product and presentation.

Starting with the public product ensures the entire unit has a clear purpose and direction, which keeps learners motivated and focused throughout the process.

Misconceptions About Public Products

One of the biggest misconceptions about public products is that they must be grandiose, a huge event with community-wide impact every single time. Let me be the first to say: That's simply not true!

A successful public product doesn't have to involve elaborate productions or massive audiences. It's about creating opportunities for students to share their work in a way that feels authentic and achievable, whether it's a small gathering of family members or a broader community showcase.

Ideas for Public Products and Authentic Audiences

Here are some examples of different public products that you can incorporate into your units:

- **Publishing a Book:** Students write and illustrate a book that becomes available for checkout in the school or local library.
- **Creating a Mural:** Collaborate with a local artist to design and paint a mural unveiled at a community event.
- **Fundraising:** Host a fundraiser for a local cause, tying learning to real-world impact.

- **Museum Tours:** Design artifacts and lead guided tours for classmates, families, or peers.
- **Performances:** Write and perform a play or musical at an assembly or community event.
- **Call-to-Action Posters:** Create awareness posters displayed in the community or submitted to a local newspaper.
- **Informational Pamphlets:** Develop brochures about a relevant topic and make them available at a local business.
- **Documentaries:** Record a short film to share with friends, family, or even online.
- **Art Walks:** Produce art inspired by a studied artist and organize an art walk for family and friends.
- **Video Presentations:** Record students filming a commercial, doing a public service announcement (PSA), or even just filming their oral presentation for family and friends that cannot attend.

As they share their learning, parents have a list of questions they can use to help guide the presentation.

Scaling Your Public Product

Not every public product has to be a large-scale production. Start small:

- Publish a poster and invite families to see it.
- Record students reading their book and share the video with relatives.

Over time, as you and your students grow more comfortable with PBL, you can work up to larger-scale exhibitions with multiple elements and broader audiences. The key is to design public products and exhibitions that match your capacity and your students' needs.

To prepare students for the real world, it's important to vary both the type of product and the format of the exhibition. Switch things up:

- Different audience sizes, from one-on-one presentations to larger groups.
- Solo work, partnerships, small groups, or large ensembles.

Each variation helps build different skills, from public speaking and teamwork to creative problem-solving and self-confidence.

A student's diorama of a pond habitat for a frog out of recycled materials.

Reflection

When people think about reflection in a Project-Based Learning (PBL) unit, they often picture it as a quick wrap-up at the very end, or worse, skip it altogether to dive into the next big thing. But reflection isn't just a nice-to-have or an afterthought; it's a key pillar of PBL that should be happening continuously. Why? Because reflection is the engine that drives improvement, deepens understanding, and polishes student work throughout the entire process.

In a PBL unit, reflection isn't something you tack on at the finish line. It's an ongoing process that's woven into every stage of inquiry and creation. Learners reflect on their research, their findings, the quality of their products, and even their peers' contributions. It's what helps them identify what's working, what's not, and how they can level up.

Reflection also plays a critical role at the conclusion of a project. It's the moment to step back and assess:

- How well did their final product answer the Driving Question?
- Was the product impactful and effective in solving the posed problem?
- What would they do differently next time?

Reflection isn't just important, it's transformative. Yet, it's one of the most frequently overlooked elements in PBL. So, how do you make sure it doesn't fall by the wayside? By building reflection into your unit from start to finish.

Why Reflection Matters

Reflection is what keeps PBL dynamic. It allows learners to pause, think critically about their process, and make intentional changes that elevate their work. It's also a space for students to recognize and celebrate their growth, not just in the final product but in the journey itself.

When you build reflection into your PBL unit, you're teaching learners a lifelong skill: how to evaluate their efforts, learn from feedback, and continuously improve. And that's a superpower they'll carry far beyond your classroom.

So, don't save reflection for the end, sprinkle it throughout the unit and watch your students' thinking, collaboration, and creativity soar.

Integrating Reflection

Reflection can take many forms and incorporating it throughout your unit can be both simple and impactful. Here are some practical ways to weave reflection into your PBL:

- **Schema Mapping:** Begin by mapping out prior knowledge and generating questions at the start of the unit. As the project progresses, reflect on those initial questions. What have you discovered? What new questions have emerged?

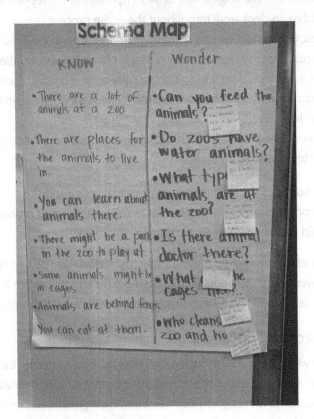

Students revisit their schema map and questions to identify new learning.

- **Peer Feedback:** Regularly give and receive feedback from peers. Use that feedback to evaluate the quality of products or ideas and make improvements.
- **Audience Surveys:** After the final exhibition, collect feedback from the audience using surveys. Discuss the results together as a group to uncover strengths and areas for growth.

- **Panel Presentations:** Before the final exhibition, invite community experts for a practice presentation. Their feedback can be invaluable for refining the product and presentation.
- **Journaling:** Keep a reflection journal throughout the unit. Use prompts to encourage learners to think critically about their progress, challenges, and next steps.
- **Group Discussions:** After hitting key milestones, gather as a group to evaluate where the project stands, what's next, and what adjustments need to be made.
- **Rubrics:** Use rubrics (a.k.a. organized checklists) to set clear expectations for products and presentations. Build in opportunities for self-assessment and reflection at multiple points along the way.

Now that we've explored the seven essential elements of Project-Based Learning, it's clear how each one plays a vital role in creating meaningful, engaging, and impactful learning experiences. From crafting a strong Driving Question to designing a public product, these elements work together to ensure students aren't just going through the motions, they're actively engaged in real learning that matters. When all the pieces come together, the classroom becomes a place where curiosity thrives, collaboration deepens, and learning feels connected to the real world.

As you take this knowledge and apply it to your own teaching, remember that PBL isn't about getting everything perfect from the start; instead, it's about diving in, trying things out, and growing along the way. Start where you are, build on what works, and don't be afraid to adjust as you go. The more you integrate these elements, the more you'll see students take ownership of their learning, think critically, and develop the skills they need beyond the classroom. And most importantly, you'll see them realize that their ideas, voices, and efforts truly matter.

So, what's next? It's time to take everything you've learned and put it into action. The next chapter is packed with 52 step-by-step PBL units, thoughtfully crafted and ready for you to adapt to meet the needs and interests of your learners. Whether you're new to PBL or a seasoned pro looking for fresh ideas, these units will guide you through the process, sparking inspiration and helping you bring PBL to life in your classroom.

02 Math Centered PBL Units

Math is all around us: in the way we count our rock collection, sort our toys, and build towers out of blocks. But for young children, math isn't just about numbers on a page; it's about exploring, discovering, and making sense of the world. Project-Based Learning (PBL) brings math to life by weaving it into hands-on, meaningful experiences that feel like play. Instead of math being abstract, children engage in real-world problem-solving, using math in ways that feel natural and exciting.

The following units are designed to help preschool and kindergarten learners build foundational math skills—like counting, sorting, measuring, money, and recognizing patterns—through creative, student-driven projects. Whether they're setting up a store, building bridges, or exploring patterns in nature, these developmentally appropriate project units make math interactive, engaging, and fun!

Jr. Chefs

Driving Question: How can we create a cookbook that celebrates food, culture, and creativity?	Public Product: The culmination of the project will be the production of a classroom cookbook that show-cases all the students' recipes. This cookbook will be shared with families and school community, providing a tangible product that celebrates the students' hard work and creativity.

Unit Overview: This project connects students with their personal and cultural backgrounds through food. It allows them to explore what different foods mean to themselves and their families. Students will investigate various cultural foods by interviewing family members and researching family recipes. They will explore the ingredients, cooking methods, and the significance of each dish, prompting questions such as, "What makes a recipe special?" and "How do different cultures use food to celebrate?" Students will have the opportunity to choose the recipes they want to include in the cookbook, allowing them to connect with their family's heritage or their personal favorites. They will design their own recipe cards, cookbook pages, and prepare their dish for others to enjoy.

Launch Event: Bring in a variety of spices, seasonings, and cultural ingredients with distinct tastes and smells. Have students taste test and smell the different ingredients and discuss if any seem familiar to them, if they can name any of them, or if they know what kinds of food they may find them in.

Module 1: What does food mean to our family?

Activities:

1. Students will begin by designing an interview to conduct with their family to learn about foods that are special to their family, have a significant meaning, have cultural relevance, are used for a specific celebration or event, etc. Some example questions include: "What was a favorite dish you ate growing up?", "What foods are important to eat for different holidays we celebrate?", "What are some important ingredients we use to make a lot of our foods?", etc.

2. After conducting the interviews, create a chart to compare the different foods they learned about. Compare important elements: what culture the dish represents, types of ingredients the dishes incorporate, specific tools or cooking methods needed, holidays or celebrations the food is made for, etc.
3. Have students journal about a food that is significant to them. A food that they love, have fond memories about, enjoy having for holidays and celebrations, etc. Have them illustrate and label a detailed picture of this dish, write about it, and share it with their classmates. Add these foods to the chart as well.

Module 2: What makes up a recipe?

Activities:

1. Students will bring copies of recipe cards from home featuring family recipes and favorite meals. Compare and contrast the recipe cards and the element included on the recipe cards.
2. Co-create a recipe card template that students will use to create their own recipe cards throughout the unit.
3. Set up an expedition to a local grocery store that has ingredients from many cultures or set up multiple small expeditions to local cultural grocery stores. Explore the different ingredients that students charted from their recipes and create a list of what some of those ingredients cost.
4. Invite a few family members or community members to do a cooking demonstration of a cultural dish. Showing students how to prepare foods using the ingredients and methods they have been researching.
5. Using a simple, no-cook recipe, have pairs or small groups of students follow the step-by-step directions on the recipe card to prepare a small dish.
6. Now that students have experienced following a recipe card, have observed others cooking traditional dishes, and have investigated family recipe cards, use the co-created recipe card template to create their own recipe card for a family favorite dish or their own personal favorite.

(Continued)

Module 3: How can we make a cookbook?

Activities:

1. Bring in a variety of cookbooks or magazines with recipes in them. Have students look through the pages and make a list of elements of cookbook pages that they see as a common thread: ingredients list, measurements/amounts, step-by-step instructions, pictures of the dish, etc.

2. Co-create a cookbook page template that students will use to turn their recipe card into a cookbook page.

3. Students will then use their recipe card to help them complete a cookbook page for the class cookbook. Include a drawing or, if they can get one, a photograph of the meal they are writing about. Make several copies of the class cookbook for the exhibition event. Have students design covers for the books as well.

4. Have students write invitations to family and community members, including those you learned from during expeditions and guest visits, inviting them to your exhibition day. Create a fun title for your celebration. Send out invitations.

5. Gather donations of ingredients for students to prepare small batches of some of their recipes, and/or ask for families to send in small batches of the recipes for the student exhibition.

Exhibition Event:

1. Host your exhibition and celebration of cultural foods where families and community members will get to sample the different dishes and learn from students about the significance and meaning behind the foods they are tasting.

2. During the celebration also have copies of the classroom cookbooks available for guests to look at and take home. In addition, you could have donations available for the cookbooks to then use the funds to contribute to a local food bank or community meal center.

Stations are set up for students to create different recipes and enjoy for snack.

Students follow recipes to make dishes to enjoy together.

Adapting for smaller learning environments: For homeschooling, co-ops, and micro school settings with fewer students, individual students can research a variety of meals and create a mini cookbook that includes a food from the following categories: a breakfast dish, lunch dish, dinner dish, desert, holiday meal, and their favorite meal. They can prepare one or more of these foods for a family meal where they can share their learning and cookbook/recipe cards and can also collect donations of food to contribute to a community outreach facility.

I Know My Numbers!

Driving Question: How can we create a tool for our classroom that will help us learn and remember our numbers?	Public Product: Students will create a classroom number line that can be used throughout the year to reference during math. Number lines will show digits, number name, quantity, ten frame representation, and pictures of student hands showing the number value.

Unit Overview: Throughout this unit, students will be introduced to and become masters of the numbers 1 through 10. Students will explore numbers and their value, learn about their digit representation and number name, and how to represent the number quantity in multiple different ways. They will be creating a class number line that they will be able to reference throughout the school year that will aid in their mathematical thinking and learning.

Launch Event: Prior to beginning this unit, remove all representations of numbers from the classroom. This could include premade number lines, 100 charts, calendars, posters, etc. When students arrive in the classroom, ask them if they notice if anything is missing. Once they noticed that everything that has to do with numbers is gone, explain to them they will need to be the ones that become the number masters and create the materials that they will need in their classroom for them to know their numbers.

Module 1: How do we count?

Activities:

1. Each day that you sit down to start your math block and work on this project unit, take time to open with a number-centered read aloud, such as 10 Red Dots, Chicka Chicka 123, Anno's Counting Book, etc. Use these books as an opportunity for students to practice, counting within 10, touching and identifying in digits and pairing them with number, names, and counting quantities.

2. Slowly introduce one to two different digits each day. Make sure students are learning the name of the number, what the number looks like, how to write the number using correct writing pathways, how to count to that number, and how to use manipulatives to show the quantity of that number. This portion of the unit will take multiple days or weeks to complete as you introduce each number and build mastery.

3. Set up a number exploration day where there are different centers or stations for students to interact with numbers. Some station or center activity ideas include a sensory bin where they will use tweezers to pick out a number manipulative and match it to a number flash card. Use Play-Doh mats where students will draw a number flashcard and then place that many balls of Play-Doh onto the mat. Count and clip cards where students will count a quantity and then place a clothespin on the corresponding number. And a station where they will use number manipulatives or flashcards to put numbers in numerical order.

Module 2: What can numbers look like?

Activities:

1. Now that students are familiar with the number, names, digits, counting, and how to write the number, introduce a variety of ways that numbers can be represented. To start with, have students practice, drawing a representation of a number. This will include showing them a digit or verbally saying a digit, and then being able to draw a quantity, such as five flowers, seven hearts, two butterflies.

2. Next, introduce the concept of a 10 frame. Using 10 frame mats and math cubes, have students practice building the quantity associated with a digit on their 10 frame teaching them how to always start in the upper left-hand corner filling in the first row of five before they jump down to the second row of five starting in the left-hand corner.

3. Build fluency with number representation on fingers with students. When calling out a number verbally or showing them a number, flashcards should build automaticity on being able to show that number on their fingers and alternatively, be able to see a representation of numbers on someone else's hands and be able to call out the value of that number.

(Continued)

Module 3: How can I help my classmates remember their numbers?

Activities:

1. Assign each student or pairs of students to a specific number that will be on the number line. Begin by having students write the digit and write or trace the number name on the number line poster template.

2. Next have students draw or use stickers to represent the quantity of their number in a 10 frame and add that to their number poster.

3. Then have students draw a quantity representation of their number, such as drawing seven cars for the number seven, or five pumpkins for the number five.

4. Finally, have students take a photograph of their hands, showing the numerical representation using their fingers. Print these off and attach them to the poster as well.

5. Once all elements are on their poster, send it through a laminator for longevity.

Exhibition Event: Have a number line ceremony where all the groups of students present their number poster and talks about the number name, the writing pathway of the number, how they chose to represent it on their 10 frame, the quantity, and what it looks like, represented on their hands. After the groups have all presented work together to put the number line in order and hang it up in a prominent spot in the learning space.

Each day students work on a new number to compile into a numbers book.

Counting collections help students connect quantity to numbers.

Adapting for smaller learning environments: For homeschooling, co-ops, and micro school settings with fewer students, individual students can create each of the number posters throughout the unit. As you spend time on each number, they can create the poster for that specific number. Then, at the end of the unit, they can hang their number line in their learning space, and/or make it into a number book if there is not room for a permanent number line for the school year.

Let's Make Money

| Driving Question: How can we create and run our own small businesses to meet the needs and wants of our community? | Public Product: Students will host a Maker's Market event where they can sell their products or offer their services to classmates, family, members, and community members. They will be responsible for advertising, running the market, handling the money, and cleaning up the event. |

Unit Overview: In this unit, students will embark on an exciting journey to become young entrepreneurs. They will explore the concepts of entrepreneurship money management, marketing, and running a business through hands-on activities and collaborations. They will create their own small businesses culminating with a Maker's Market where they can showcase and sell their products or services to their classmates and community members.

Launch Event: Bring in local small business owners that can come in and share with students their experience of starting a business, running a business, and some of the unique challenges that come with running their own business. Then have them challenge the students to create their own small business, thus launching the project.

Module 1: What can I offer my community?

Activities:

1. Begin by having a brainstorming session, or students can share ideas for things they can create or services that they can provide to their community. Encourage creativity and collaboration prompting them to think about what products or services that they enjoy that they could also offer someone else.

2. Introduce students to market research by having them conduct simple market research by asking family members, classmates, or other individuals around the school about their interests and things that they like and need to buy. After they conduct that research, create a class chart to record what they discovered.

3. Next, have students begin to create a business plan. This should include a business name that is catchy and will spark someone's interest in their business, a product or service description explaining what they're going to sell or provide to the community, and a target market audience explaining who their primary customers will be or who they are trying to sell to.

4. Then they will also need to create a simple budget for their business, including costs of materials. They will need to research the price of their products either online, by going to stores with their families or on an expedition and decide how much they will need to charge for their product or service based on the amount of money they will have to spend to create the product.

5. Encourage students to reach out to family members, neighbors, and community members as well as local businesses to ask for donations of supplies as well.

Module 2: How will others find my business?

Activities:

1. Once their business plan is in place, they will now need to think about how they're going to get the word out about their Maker's Market and their individual business. Have students look at newspapers, magazines, and local advertisements for different businesses in the area discussing the different elements of flyers and advertisements that they might want to include in their own.

2. Have students create flyers, posters, and advertisements to promote their individual business, as well as create a flyer for the Maker's Market as a whole. Encourage them to think about color, imagery, and catchy phrases that could attract customers.

3. Select a time, date and location for the makers, market and distribute the flyers throughout the school, send them home with families, and find local businesses or community locations where the flyers can be hung up.

(Continued)

Module 3: How can I run a market?

Activities:

1. Set aside time for students to create their products and prepare their services for the Maker's Market day. Encourage them to think about the quality of the product that they are creating.
2. Work together as a team to design the Maker's Market experience. How will the space be laid out, what materials will they need for that day such as tables, tablecloths, change boxes, etc.
3. Create signs, price tags, decorations, etc., for the day of the Maker's Market.
4. Spend time role-playing customers and interactions and teaching students about customer service and how to interact with the people that will come to the Maker's Market. Role-play various scenarios where they can practice greeting customers, answering questions, and making sales. This will include how to use a calculator to figure out how to give back exact change. Encourage students to price their materials that they are selling in even amounts of $.50 to full dollar amounts to make the counting change back process easier.

Exhibition Event: On the day of the Maker's Market, have the students set up and decorate for the market, including setting up their individual business tables, their products, along with their price tags. As customers arrive, have students greet the customers and welcome them to their Maker's Market and man their individual tables for the duration of the market. When the market is complete, students should clean up the market and count their earnings. Decide as a class how the earnings from the market will be distributed and what those funds will be used for, such as class expeditions, donating to a meaningful community organization, having a class party to celebrate.

Adapting for smaller learning environments: For homeschooling, co-ops, and micro school settings with fewer students, individual students can create a small business that they can advertise to their family, friends, and neighborhood. Have students create flyers and pass them out throughout their neighborhood advertising the day they will have their small business set up similar to a lemonade stand type scenario. You can also have students connect with pre-established, local makers, markets, craft fairs, or small business events, and potentially host a booth during one of those community events.

Block City

Driving Question: What important places are in a city that help it thrive?	Public Product: Students will create a city using unit blocks and create roads, street signs, business signs, and labels, etc., to enhance their block city. They will take others on a guided tour of their city, talking about each of the creations and why it is important to have in their block city.

Unit Overview: In this unit, preschoolers will embark on a creative journey to design and construct a block city that represents their community through hands-on activities. Students will explore essential community elements, such as schools, parks, hospitals, and shops while developing teamwork and problem-solving skills they will collaboratively plan their city layout, build structures using unit blocks and create signs and labels for each building. The combination of the unit will involve a guided tour of their block city where they will showcase their work to family members explaining the importance of each of the structures and the roles that they play in their community.

Launch Event: To kick off this unit, take students on a walking tour of a community hub in your town. Have them notice and take pictures of prominent community buildings and locations that they see on their walk, such as parks, benches, community spaces, libraries, grocery stores, fire stations.

Module 1: What makes up a city?

Activities:

1. After the launch event, bring back the photographs that students took and their observations and create an anchor chart that compiles all they noticed on their city walk. Engage with picture books, reading aloud, or short video clips about communities that can engage students and provide visual examples of additional community elements that may have not been seen on your city walk. Add those additional examples to the anchor chart.
2. Introduce students to different types and styles of buildings found in the community, such as a school, a hospital, a fire station, a grocery store, etc. create a visual chart with pictures and names of these buildings for students to reference during this unit.

(Continued)

3. Talk about the shapes that they noticed in different types of buildings that they've seen in their community or in pictures and videos that they have observed in class. Using unit blocks, encourage students to begin trying out different ways to create these structures and shapes using teamwork and collaboration.

Module 2: What do we need in our city?

Activities:

1. Now let the students in on the secret that they will actually be creating their very own city out of blocks. Begin by having them identify what key buildings and places they would want in their very own city. It is common for kids to include places like candy stores, toy stores, parks, and play-grounds, and those are all great elements for them to include in their block city, but encourage them to include essential buildings like hospitals and schools and neighborhoods that would benefit a lot of people that live in their city.
2. Once a list of essential places and buildings have been established, assign individual or small groups of students to those various buildings and places and have them begin to experiment designing how they will represent or build it out of unit blocks. Have students photograph their creations so they can easily rebuild.
3. Utilizing the photographs they took and work together to create a large map of the city. Discuss the locations of buildings and spaces in relation to where people live work play and learn. Using a large piece of butcher paper or poster board, draw out the city to scale, indicating where each building will be built, where roads will be, benches, stop signs, etc.

Module 3: How will people know where they are at in the city?

Activities:

1. Now that the map is created, have students take time to design the other elements needed for their city, such as signs for their buildings, that they will need to write, draw, and/or color to let people know where they are.
2. Work together to decide on different street names and have students write, trace, or dictate the names of the streets and add them to their city map.
3. Have students work together to draw, color, paint, sculpt, or create differ-ent elements to add to their block city, such as trees, ponds, shrubs, wildlife that could be found in their community.

4. Have students use their pictures to guide their re-creation of their buildings and place them in the appropriate places designated on their city map and attach the signs they created for their structure as well.

5. Have students prepare for the city tour by deciding how they want to guide others through their block city. Discuss what they'll say to the family members and community members and how they will guide them through the city, highlighting important features and buildings.

Exhibition Event: Host a special event where students will invite family members, siblings, or other classes throughout the school to tour their block city. Have students take turns being the tour guides, explaining each building and its purpose and pointing out the different signs and labels and elements that they created and contributed to their classes block city.

Students plan buildings and places they want to include in their city.

Unit blocks are used to replicate familiar buildings in their city.

Adapting for smaller learning environments: For homeschooling, co-ops, and micro school settings with fewer students, individual students can spend time researching the different city elements and design and create their own block city independently or with a partner, rather than different groups taking on different elements. Instead, they would be responsible for completing an entire block city themselves.

My Learning Space

Driving Question: What does a classroom learning space look like that reflects our needs and interests while making it a fun and inviting place to learn?	Public Product: Students will host an open house night, where they will give tours of their newly designed learning space and talk about why they included different elements and how it will help them learn and stay engaged throughout the school year.

Unit Overview: Throughout this unit, students will collaborate to design and arrange their own classroom learning space. They will explore the various areas necessary for a functional and inviting classroom, such as reading corners, art stations, play areas, individual and group learning spaces. They will work together to create a floorplan, arrange furniture, and design labels and signs for designated areas of the learning space to ensure that their classroom reflects their needs and interests. The culmination of this unit will be an open house event where they will give tours to family members to showcase their personalized learning environment, explaining the purpose of each space.

Launch Event: Prior to student arrival, remove as much furniture as possible from the classroom learning space and or stack or move it off to the side so when students enter, they see a somewhat blank slate. Have a question posted on the board or in a central meeting area, such as "what should a classroom look like?" to begin thinking and instigate student conversation prior to group discussion.

Module 1: What does a classroom need?

Activities:

1. Gather together and brainstorm and record student schema surrounding what they believe to be true about what should be found in a class-room setting.
2. Have a variety of books that showcase different classrooms, including nonfiction examples or even fictional classrooms represented in picture books, and have students use Post-it notes to make a note of elements they see in the classrooms that they are drawn to.

3. Have them share with the group these different classroom elements that they observed and add those Post-it notes to the anchor chart.
4. Make a list of the type of people who are served in classrooms, including students, students with different needs and abilities, students with different mobility needs, adults that enter and use the classroom, etc.

Module 2: What should our classroom look like?

Activities:

1. Have a discussion with students about the different types of learning that will take place in the classroom that year. Create a poster that has a different section marked off for each of these content areas, such as math, writing, art, group projects, individual learning time, reading.
2. Have students brainstorm and make a list in each of those sections about the types of furniture, elements, and needs necessary to accommodate the learning that is happening. Make sure and discuss the furniture that is available to include in their classroom design plans.
3. Have students work independently or with a partner or small group to create rough draft sketches of different areas that could be included in the classroom or an entire classroom layout. Bring these different layouts together and tape them up so they can be observed by the whole group and discuss different elements that people included that the group likes and would like to implement or how elements from different versions can be combined into the final layout.

Module 3: How can we create our own learning space?

Activities:

1. Either assign groups of students separate areas to create floor plans based off the final decisions made by the whole group of what should be included in those learning spaces or work as a whole group to create a floor plan for the entire classroom altogether. Then bring the plans together to create a full map of how the classroom will be set up.
2. Work together to arrange furniture and classroom elements to match the floor plans created.
3. Create decorations, signs, and labels for the different areas of the classroom.
4. Create invitations to bring home to families, inviting them to an open house event.

(Continued)

Exhibition Event: Students will host an open house event for families invited to tour the newly designed classroom. Students will act as tour guide showcasing their learning space explaining the purpose of each area and how they designed it. Have students take turns explaining their favorite area of the classroom and what activities will be taking place there.

Students identify that they need a coat tree and shoe bench in their entryway.

A quiet calm down space is created for students to take breaks. They selected items for a quiet basket.

Adapting for smaller learning environments: For homeschooling, co-ops, and micro school settings with fewer students, individual students can design their learning spaces on a smaller scale. What would make a conducive learning space for them within their home environment? How can they take a community use space and make it their own while they use it for learning? Can they design a mobile classroom cart that can provide for all their needs when they are learning and then be moved out of the space when it is in use for something else?

Itsy Bitsy Spider

Driving Question: What shapes and patterns can we discover in the webs of spiders?	Public Product: Students will create a spiderweb-inspired art installation that will be displayed in a public location for others to learn from and enjoy.

Unit Overview: Throughout this unit, students will dive into the world of spiders and their intricate webs. Through hands-on activities and exploration, students will learn about different types of spiderwebs, examining the shapes and patterns that make each design unique. Students will engage in creative projects, such as crafting their own spiderwebs using various materials and techniques, and the unit will culminate in a spiderweb-inspired art installation that they will display in a centralized area for their community to enjoy.

Launch Event: Kick off this unit with the spider discovery day where students will explore the outdoor environment for real spiderwebs. Provide magnifying glasses for students to observe the webs closely, encouraging them to notice the different shapes and patterns they see in the web. Provide opportunities for students to snap photos of the webs that they find to bring back for discussion in the classroom.

Module 1: What are spiders and how do they make webs?

Activities:

1. Bring the pictures of Spider-Man webs that students took in the natural environment back into the classroom to discuss the different shapes and patterns and lines that they see in the pictures.
2. Engage in research through nonfiction books about spiders, as well as observing additional photographs and watching short clips of spiders creating webs.
3. Using a ball of yarn, have students stand in a circle and call out a class-mate's name. Have them hold onto the end of the yarn and throw the yarn ball across the circle to another classmate whose name they called out. That classmate will hold onto the yarn, call on another classmate, and toss the yarn ball to that child. Have this continue until every student has been tossed the yarn ball. Then have them pull the yarn tight and snap a photo of the spiderweb that they created.

(Continued)

Module 2: What types of spiderwebs are there?
Activities: 1. Research different types of spiderwebs, such as orb webs, funnel webs, sheet webs, cobwebs, and triangle webs. Research different types of spiderwebs, such as orb webs, funnel webs, sheet webs, cobwebs, triangle webs. Create an anchor chart where students match a picture of a web to the correct label of the type of web that it is. 2. Investigate what types of spiders make these different types of webs and why and how the different types of webs are useful to the spiders that make them.

Module 3: What shapes, lines, and patterns can I use to create my own web?
Activities: 1. Learn about and name different 2-D shapes, types of lines, such as straight and curved, and how to recognize patterns in pictures. 2. Create a shape exploration stations day where students can explore building shapes using a variety of elements. Station ideas include pattern blocks, geoboards with rubber bands, weaving, looms with yarn, wax sticks, using Play-Doh, etc. 3. Have students select the type of spiderweb they find the most intriguing or beautiful. Using wax paper, white yarn, craft glue, and Mod Podge, have students use a permanent marker to design their style of spider web on the wax paper. Then use a thin layer of Mod Podge painted onto the wax paper and pieces of yarn cut to length laid on top of the black marker showing through. Once it is adhered to the wax paper, use another layer of Mod Podge over the top. Once it has dried and the yarn has hardened gently remove the hardened spiderweb from the wax paper. Hang the spiderwebs together in a community centered location.
Exhibition Event: Student spiderwebs should be hung in a community center location, such as a community center, commons area at the school, children's library where others can enjoy the beauty of the patterns and shapes seen in the spiderwebs that students created.

Adapting for smaller learning environments: For homeschooling, co-ops, and micro school settings with fewer students, individual students can create a spider web for each of the types of webs studies and hang their art installation in a public space for others to enjoy.

Building Bridges

Driving Question: How can we design and build a bridge? Will it be strong enough to hold the weight of a toy truck?	Public Product: Students will design and construct their own bridges, testing their strength and structural integrity by placing the weight of a medium size toy truck on the bridge.

Unit Overview: Throughout this unit, students will learn about the various types of bridges, including beam bridges, arch, bridges, suspension bridges, and truss bridges. They will examine the function of those types of bridges as well as key structural elements. Students will develop an understanding of the engineering concepts and importance of bridges and connecting communities. The unit will culminate in a creative challenge where students will design and construct their own bridge and will test the structural integrity and strength of their bridge by placing a medium sized toy truck on it and seeing if it withstands the weight.

Launch Event: Obtain a letter from a local engineer, challenging the students to create a bridge that will hold the weight of a medium sized toy truck. Have the toy truck available for students to pick up and feel the weight of the truck. In the letter have the engineer specify a deadline for the bridge creation, and the date that they will come to the classroom to test their bridges.

Module 1: What types of bridges connect communities?

Activities:

1. Print off pictures of a variety of types of bridges, including famous bridges and ones local to their community. Hang them in a central meeting area. Have students observe the bridges and make statements about things that they notice about the bridges. This could include shapes, structural elements, similarities, and differences between different bridges, etc. Use Post-it notes to record their thinking and fix them to the picture of the bridge they are discussing.

2. Using nonfiction books, video clips, and other articles or images, introduce students to the various types of bridges, such as beam bridges, arch bridges, suspension bridges, and truss bridges. Create an anchor chart that highlights the key elements of each type of bridge, where, and for what they are built, and sort the pictures of bridges from the prior activity into the bridge categories.

(Continued)

Module 2: How are bridges built?
Activities:
1. Have students brainstorm questions they have for an expert who has experience in designing bridges for communities.
2. Host a guest speaker, such as a civil engineer or architect, discuss the importance of bridges, and share real world examples of bridges they have designed and worked on in the community.
3. Have students explore building bridge structures, using simple materials like blocks, popsicle sticks, toothpicks, and straws, etc. Discuss the key structural elements of bridges, including their supports, beams, and tension while they create these small models.
Module 3: Can I create a bridge that won't fall under the weight of a toy truck?
Activities:
1. Now that students have explored building small bridge models, it is time for them to think about their bridge design that will hold up a medium-sized toy truck as challenged at the beginning of the unit. Have students draw designs for their bridge using elements that they have learned about through their research and from their guest speaker and create a list of materials that they will need to build these bridges from a list provided, including things like cardboard, craft sticks, string, etc.
2. Provide student work time to work independently, in pairs, or in small groups to follow their plans and use the provided materials to create the bridge that they designed.
3. Write a classroom invitation to the local engineer who challenged the students from the beginning of the unit during the launch event, inviting them to come to their bridge testing exhibition.
Exhibition Event: Students will present their bridges and discuss the elements of their design and what type of bridge they chose to create. Have them talk about why they think their bridge will hold up to the size and weight of a medium-sized toy truck. Then have the guest engineer place the truck on the bridge to see if it will hold up to the weight. After the exhibition, have students gather to reflect about their experience building and testing their bridge and if their bridge was successful, why they think it was successful, and if it was unsuccessful, what changes they could make if they were to test their bridge again.

Adapting for smaller learning environments: For homeschooling, co-ops, and micro school settings with fewer students, individual students can create a bridge in individually rather than in a small group or with a partner. You could also go on an expedition to a local engineer firm to learn in their environment.

Gamify It

Driving Question: How can we create a fun game that helps our friends practice and master important math skills?	Public Product: Students will create a game that will target a specific math skill they are currently mastering, and they will showcase their games to their classmates and allow other others to play them.

Unit Overview: In this unit, students will identify a specific math skill they are currently working on such as addition, subtraction, counting, or shape recognition. They will explore game design elements, brainstorm ideas, and create their games using a variety of materials. Students will have a game showcase where their classmates will be able to play the different games and practice their math skills.

Launch Event: Have a variety of popular games, such as Candyland, Chutes and Ladders, Hi Ho Cherry-o, Go Fish. laid out throughout the classroom. Allow students to rotate through playing these different games.

Module 1: What makes a good game?

Activities:

1. After students have rotated through and played the different games, gather and discuss what makes a game fun and engaging. Create a list of the different game elements that students enjoyed most while playing.
2. Create a visual chart showing the different elements that make up a game, such as the game board, game pieces, spinners, dice, playing cards.
3. Have students reflect on the math skills they're currently learning or have already mastered or been practicing in class. Guide them to choose one specific skill to focus on for their game, such as counting, addition, identifying shapes.
4. Encourage students to begin brainstorming ideas for games that incorporate their chosen math skill and encourage collaboration, allowing students to work together and combine their ideas into one cohesive game concept.

(Continued)

Module 2: How can I create a game that is fun to play?

Activities:

1. Have students begin to design their game concept by identifying elements from other games they enjoy that they would like to incorporate into their new math game. This could be things like using colored game squares like in Candyland, drawing cards to show the number of spaces moved like in the game Sorry, spinning a spinner to collect items like in Hi Ho Cherry-o, etc.
2. Have students draw out plans for their game, such as the game board, how they want their game pieces to look, card, design.
3. Provide students with materials, such as cardboard, markers, dice, glue, card stock, etc. to begin designing their games and game pieces.
4. Provide time for students to test out the games that they created them-selves to check for engagement, focus on the math skill, and to work out any elements of the game that could be too confusing for players to understand.

Module 3: Is my game ready for others to play?

Activities:

1. Now that the games are complete and have been played by the creators, it is time for them to create the rulebook for their games. Have students write or dictate the rules and steps to playing their game, encouraging them to keep them simple and clear so that other players can easily play their game.
2. Organize a game testing day where students can play games with one other team and provide constructive feedback. Encourage them to think about what they liked, what could be improved, how well the game helped them practice the math skill, or if anything was confusing while playing.
3. Provide students opportunities to use the feedback that they were given to make alterations to their game and their game rules.

Exhibition Event: Host a math game showcase where students will invite their classmates to play their games. Have one member of the game creation team stay with the game to explain it to the players. Have students rotate who is in charge of running their game so each student has the opportunity to show-case their game and play a few games that others made.

Adapting for smaller learning environments: For homeschooling, co-ops, and micro school settings with fewer students, individual students can create their own game and connect with a local library or community center and ask to bring their game to be available for others to play.

Seeing Shapes

Driving Question: What shapes do we see in the world around us?	Public Product: Students will create a poster for different 2-D and 3-D shapes that will have a collage of photographs they have taken of those shapes represented in the real world and in nature.

Unit Overview: In this unit, students will explore and understand 2-D and 3-D shapes in their environment. Students will identify different shapes and photograph various shapes found in the world and nature. They will learn about the characteristics of shapes, such as their sides corners and curves, while developing their observational skills. Students will design shape posters that show a case their photographs of the shapes that they discovered highlighting the beauty of geometry in their everyday life.

Launch Event: Provide students with a checklist of common 2-D and 3-D shapes. Take a clipboard and a pen or pencil on a scavenger hunt through the classroom, school, or the playground and find items that are representative of those shapes.

Module 1: What are 2-D shapes?

Activities:

1. Introduce students to 2-D shapes, such as circles, squares, triangles, and rectangles. Have students describe the shapes, name the shapes, and classify shapes based on their attributes.
2. Provide hands-on opportunities for students to build and manipulate shapes. This could include building shapes out of Play-Doh, with popsicle sticks, with pattern blocks, and practicing tracing and drawing shapes.
3. Introduce students to additional 2-D shapes, such as trapezoid, rhombus, hexagon, octagon, ellipse, pentagon, crescent, heart, semi circle, and star. Have students also describe the shapes, name them, and classify them based on their attributes as well.

(Continued)

Module 2: What are 3-D shapes?

Activities:

1. Introduce students to 3-D shapes such as spheres, cylinders, cubes, and cones. Have students describe the shapes, name the shapes, and classify the shapes based on their attributes.
2. Provide hands-on opportunities for students to build and manipulate these 3-D shapes. This could include building the shapes out of Play-Doh, with marshmallows and toothpicks, or toothpicks and cranberries.
3. Compare and contrast the difference between 2-D and 3-D shapes. Have students sort and classify shapes based on if they are 2-D or 3-D shapes.

Module 3: What shapes surround us?

Activities:

1. Provide students with cameras or tablets to take photographs of shapes they find during a nature walk, around the classroom, around the playground, as they walk through the school, or even at home. Encourage them to capture 2-D and 3-D shapes.
2. Print out the photographs that students took, and together have students work to sort them based on the shape they represent.
3. Have students work in small groups to draw and color, cut out from paper, or paint a representation of the shape they've been assigned on the top of their poster. Have them trace or write the name of the shape as well.
4. Then have them collage the photographs of their shapes represented in the world and nature onto their poster. You can encourage them to write labels for the objects to cut out and glue next to the photographs as well if they are able.

Exhibition Event: Students will host a gallery walk where friends, family, and school community can view their posters. Students will talk about the shapes that they studied and the different real world, objects, and elements of nature they were able to find that represent that shape. Students will host a gallery walk, where friends, family, and school community can view their posters. Students will talk about the shapes they studied and the different real world, objects, and elements of nature they were able to find that represent those shapes.

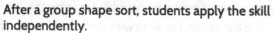

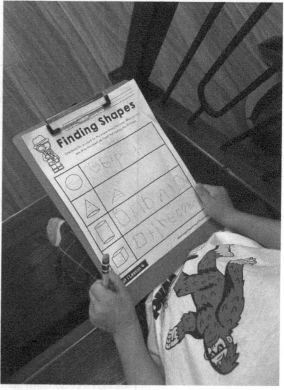

After a group shape sort, students apply the skill independently.

Students go on a scavenger hunt to record objects they find for each shape.

Adapting for smaller learning environments: For homeschooling, co-ops, and micro school settings with fewer students, individual students can create a poster that represents 2-D shapes altogether with one or two photographs of each shape found in the real world or in nature and then a separate poster of the 3-D shapes in the same way.

Plan It Out

Driving Question: How can we use what we know about clocks to create a schedule that helps us plan out our school day?	Public Product: Students will collaborate to create a classroom schedule chart. They will create labels for each part of their school day as well as auxiliary activities that happen less frequently. They will also create clock symbols that represent different times throughout the day that they will pair alongside the schedule labels as they outline their school day each morning.

Unit Overview: In this unit, students will explore the concept of telling time to the hour and half hour while learning how to create and use a daily classroom schedule. Students will gain a deeper understanding of how to read clocks and the importance of time management. They will work collaboratively to design a classroom schedule chart that outlines different learning events throughout the day. Each day, one student will be responsible for using the schedule and clock cards he or she has created to work with the teacher and fill out the daily classroom schedule, allowing the student to take ownership of the learning.

Launch Event: Have the teacher write a letter to the class explaining that they have noticed a lot of students asking the questions: What time are we doing XYZ? What's next? When do we go home? When are we having lunch? In this letter also explain that they are about to spend time studying how to read clocks and tell time, and they will be responsible for creating a class schedule and changing it each day, so that way they always know what they're doing and when throughout the school day.

Module 1: How do you read a clock?

Activities:

1. Begin by establishing an understanding of time, working on identifying and naming the time of day such as morning, afternoon or evening, day of the week, yesterday, today and tomorrow and months of the year.

2. Then introduce the clock, the parts of a clock, the different hours of a clock, and the hour and the minute hand. Work together to add labels to your classroom clock for these elements.
3. Teach students how to read both an analog and a digital clock. Focus on time to the hour and the half hour unless your schedule naturally has to break itself up by 15- or 10-minute segments. If that is the case, make sure and introduce those concepts as well.

Module 2: What are our daily routines?

Activities:

1. Discuss daily routines in the classroom and various learning events that take place throughout the day, for example a morning meeting, math time, lunch, recesses, reading. Make a list of all these daily occurrences that happen in the school day.
2. Then we begin to discuss other events that happen less frequently but still could pop up on their school schedule. These could include rotating specialist classes like art, music, PE, library time, etc. assemblies, expeditions, guest speakers, etc. Add these schedule events to the list as well in a separate color.

Module 3: How can we show what is happening and when?

Activities:

1. Decide with students what symbol can be associated with the school event that would help a non-reader be able to look at the schedule and also know what was happening next based on the symbol next to the label word. On the list you generated in Module 2, add a Post-it note next to each of the items with the symbol the student described.
2. Assign students a label to create where they can trace or independently write the label and put the symbol next to it for individuals who need a visual rather than a word to utilize the schedule.
3. Have students create small clock cards that show different times of the day that you rotate through different events. Have them show different times by the hour half hour or any other times that your day has to naturally be broken up into.

(Continued)

Exhibition Event: Rather than a large exhibition event, this project is some-thing that will continue throughout the school year. Each day, assign a student the task of the classroom schedule builder. Meet with the student and go over the schedule of events for the day and have him or her select the schedule cards for those events and put them in order in a central location, such as a pocket chart or just taped up onto the wall. Then have the student find the clock cards that go with the times of day that you have scheduled those specific learning blocks. Have him or her place those clock cards next to the labels for the schedule. Throughout the day if students ask, what is coming next or how long until something else, direct their attention to the schedule that they created with their classmates to have them take ownership of their learning and their school day.

Adapting for smaller learning environments: For homeschooling, co-ops, and micro school settings with fewer students, individual students can create each of the schedule cards and clock cards rather than have it split up amongst different students. Daily they can work with you to create their schedule and reference it as the learning day progresses.

03 Science-Centered PBL Units

Science is all about curiosity—asking questions, making discoveries, and exploring the world in new ways. Young children are natural scientists, constantly observing, experimenting, and wondering about everything around them. Project-Based Learning (PBL) taps into this innate curiosity by turning science into hands-on, meaningful experiences. Instead of simply learning facts, children engage in real-world investigations, using their senses and creativity to explore scientific concepts in ways that feel like play.

The following units are designed to help preschool and kindergarten learners build foundational science skills, such as making predictions, observing changes, exploring cause and effect, and classifying objects. We will be exploring the natural world around us, insect and animals, the weather, and more through a variety of hands-on and child-centered science explorations.

Trees and the Seasons

Driving Question: How do trees grow and thrive in different seasons?	Public Product: Students will create a tree walk with informational signs and posters that pair with native trees around the school property.

Unit Overview: Throughout this unit, students will learn all about trees, their function and purpose, the different parts of trees, and different types of trees. Students will learn about where trees grow and how trees grow and what they need to survive. They will study how trees changed throughout the season and then will create posters for different trees, native to where they live that will teach readers about the bark, the leaves or needles on the tree, the cones seeds and fruit found on the tree and how to identify the tree.

Launch Event: Gather a variety of tree elements, such as small pieces of bark, pinecones, pine needles, leaves, nuts, and seeds and lay them out on tables with magnifying glasses. Allow students to explore and investigate these nature elements.

Module 1: What are trees?

Activities:

1. Meet together and begin by creating a Know, Want, Learn (KWL) chart writing down what students already know about trees, what they want to know about trees, and leaving a space for them to record any new informa- tion that they learn about trees throughout the unit.
2. Discuss the concept of living versus nonliving by gathering pictures or objects of items that are alive and items that are in the objects. Discuss the qualities of living versus nonliving things and have students sort these objects or pictures into living versus nonliving.
3. Research through nonfiction books and pictures of trees and discuss the parts of trees and their function or purpose, such as the roots, trunk, bark branches, twigs leaves, needles, fruit, nuts, cones, and seeds. Also discuss how these elements make a tree, a deciduous or a coniferous tree.
4. Talk about where trees might grow both naturally or because they were planted by people. Talk about how different trees grow in people's yards, at the park, in cities, in the country, in the mountains, near rivers and streams, alongside lakes, and in swamps, etc.

Module 2: What do trees need to survive?

Activities:

1. Discuss the different elements that trees need to survive such as water, air, space, sunlight, and nutrients from the soil.
2. Have students act out and talk through the process of how the roots carry nutrients to the tree and the leaves use sunlight, air, and water to make food for the tree.
3. Conduct research through nonfiction books, by studying pictures, or watching short video clips about how trees changed throughout the seasons. Discuss what trees do in each season and what they might need more of or less of in different seasons, and why.

Module 3: How can we teach others about the trees that grow where we live?

Activities:

1. Assign small groups of students to native trees to your area or the types of trees that are found on the property of the school. Encourage them to research these types of trees at home with their family and bring in some of their new learning to share with the class.
2. Model for students, the difference between a fictional drawing and a scientific drawing. Model how to edit and revise their drawings as well as how to use realistic coloring versus creative coloring.
3. For each small group of students that is researching a specific tree, assign each individual in that group one element of the tree that can be used to help identify the tree, for example, the leaves, needles, the bark, the cone or seed or fruit, and one individual should also do a full drying of the tree. Using images from their research, students will draw a scientific drawing of that element of their tree to attach to the poster as well as create a label for that element of the tree.
4. Also have each student dictate trace or write their own sentence, giving one interesting fact that they learned about their tree to add to the poster as well.

Exhibition Event: Hang these posters next to the trees on the property or in a common area where individuals can go on a gallery walk or a nature tree walk and learn about each tree and how to identify it from the student made posters.

Using dried leaves, students create deciduous trees.

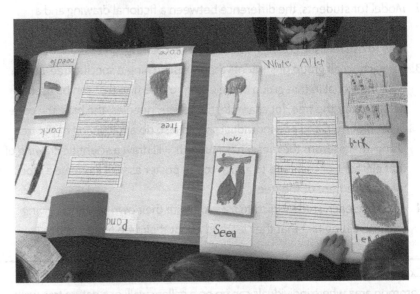

Students add their informational sentences to their tree walk posters.

Adapting for smaller learning environments: For homeschooling, co-ops, and micro school settings with fewer students, individual students can create tree identification posters for the trees growing at home or in their neighborhood. They can hang up these posters for passersby to read and learn from.

I Am a Scientist

Driving Question: What do scientists do?	Public Product: Students will earn their official certificate for becoming a scientist once they have completed all the elements required to be a scientist, such as conducting research, producing a diagram, conducting an experiment, and publishing the findings of their experiment.

Unit Overview: In this introductory unit, students will learn about important jobs that scientists must do as they research and learn about new things. Students will learn how to activate their schema, generate research questions, conduct research, dissect, create diagrams, create a hypothesis, conduct an experiment, record observations, and publish their research findings. They will do these things through a study of apples.

Launch Event: As students enter the learning space, have a variety of science tools, such as magnifying glasses, microscopes, pencils, petri, dishes, beakers laid out in the meeting space. Allow students an opportunity to interact with these materials, investigate them, and make observations.

Module 1: How do scientists know so much?

Activities:

1. The first thing that scientist do is they activate their schema, which is what they already know about the topic that they want to research. Introduce to students that the topic they're going to be researching as junior scientists is apples. Create a schema map where students will record what they already know about apples. This is the schema that they have about apples, and it can help them guide their research.

2. Have students generate questions that they have about apples. This is another important job of a scientist. They need to be able to come up with research questions in order to learn more about the subject they are studying.

(Continued)

Module 2: How can scientists learn more?

Activities:

1. One way that scientist can learn more about the subject they are studying is through research. Gather a variety of nonfiction apple books, images of apples, and watch short video clips about how apples grow and ways that they are used. Record any new learning onto their ski map and connect them to any of the research questions that they posed if they were able to answer one of their questions based on the research they have done.

2. Another way that scientist can learn more is through studying objects and dissecting. Set up a sensory experience where students can touch, taste, smell, and look at apples of different types and come up with different words and ways to describe these apples in detail.

3. Next cut up on the apples to see all of their different parts. Discuss new vocabulary, such as the skin, flesh, core, seeds, stem, and leaf.

4. Use this new knowledge of apples and their different parts to create a scientific apple diagram where students can draw, color, and label the parts of an apple.

Module 3: How can scientists teach others?

Activities:

1. An important job of a scientist is to share their learning with others so that they can grow their knowledge as well. One way to do this is through conducting experiments and sharing their findings. Start by cutting apples into slices and laying them on a plate. Discuss with students what their observations are about these apples. What do they look like? How many are there? What do they feel like and what do they smell like? Record this information on a T chart on the left-hand side, showing how these apples look the first day that they observed them.

2. Have students form what is called a hypothesis or what they think will happen to the apples if they are left out on the plate for a week. A hypothesis is an educated and research fact guess or assumption of what can happen in an experiment based on schema and research.

3. Check the apple slices daily and discuss the student's hypothesis and the observations of any changes that have happened in the apples.

4. At the end of the week, record their observations on the T chart to show how the apples changed after a week of sitting out. Discuss if their hypothesis was correct and create a final draft version of the research findings for publishing.

Exhibition Event: Students will present their research, diagrams, scientific observations, and experiment results at an exhibition event where they can invite their family, friends, and school community members.

Students paint apples to decorate for their apple party at the end of the unit.

Adapting for smaller learning environments: This project can be implemented as is for alternative learning environments and class sizes.

From Seed to Pumpkin

Driving Question: Are pumpkins more than just a decoration?	Public Product: Students will produce a pumpkin flip book that teaches about the parts of a pumpkin, how a pumpkin grows, foods made with pumpkin, how to experience a pumpkin with your senses, and facts about pumpkins. They will present these flip books to family, friends, and school community members to teach them about pumpkins as well as prepare different pumpkin foods to be taste tested.

Unit Overview: Throughout this unit, students will explore pumpkins through sensory explorations, learn about the parts of a pumpkin, what they need to grow, their life cycle, and different foods made from pumpkin. They will be creating an informational pumpkin flip book that will teach others about what they have learned about pumpkins, and they will prepare a variety of pumpkin recipes for others to taste and experience at their exhibition event.

Launch Event: Have a variety of pumpkins laid out and some cut open for students to observe, touch, explore, and investigate upon arriving to the classroom.

Module 1: What is a pumpkin?

Activities:

1. Gather together and discuss the observations that students made as they were experiencing the different pumpkins. Create an anchor chart outlining what they could see smell, feel, taste, or even hear as they were exploring the pumpkins.
2. Using one of the full pumpkins and one of the pumpkins cut in half, explore the parts of a pumpkin, such as the vine, stem, rib, skin or rind, blossom and, pulp, fibrous strands, and seeds.
3. Have students create a scientific drawing of a pumpkin and all of its parts and dictate trace or write labels to name each part of their pumpkin diagram.
4. Complete the pumpkin flip book pages that discuss the parts of a pumpkin.

Module 2: How do pumpkins grow?

Activities:

1. Discuss what pumpkins need to grow and thrive, such as sunlight, air, water, space, and nutrients from the soil. Complete the pumpkin flip book page talking about the needs of pumpkins.
2. Using nonfiction books, and short video clips, research and observe the pumpkin life cycle. Highlight each stage of a pumpkin's life cycle including the seed, sprout, plant, vine, flower, green pumpkin, and mature pumpkin stages of the life cycle. Complete the pumpkin flip book page that models the life cycle of a pumpkin and create a poster that diagrams the life cycle of a pumpkin.

Module 3: Can you use a pumpkin for more than decorating?

Activities:

1. Prepare and taste a variety of pumpkin recipes, such as cookies, pie, pumpkin seeds, bread, rolls, muffins, soup.
2. Graph and compare people's favorites and least favorites when taste testing different pumpkin recipes.
3. Complete your pumpkin flip book talking about what pumpkins can be and recording additional interesting facts that you've learned about pumpkins throughout the unit.

Exhibition Event: Prepare the most popular pumpkin recipes when the class graphed their taste test results for their guests to try. As guests arrive have students present them with different pumpkin foods to taste as well as guide them through their flip book teaching them all they learned about pumpkins throughout the unit.

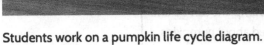

Students work on a pumpkin life cycle diagram.

Hands on manipulatives for students to build a pumpkin diagram.

Adapting for smaller learning environments: For homeschooling, co-ops, and micro school settings with fewer students, individual students can prepare a variety of pumpkin treats to present at their exhibition alongside their pumpkin flip book. They can have their guests fill out a survey about their favorite pumpkin treats that they eat that day, and after the exhibition they can use these results to graph and find out which were the most popular amongst their guests.

Feathers, Beaks, and Wings

Driving Question: Why do birds need feathers, beaks, and wings?	Public Product: Students will create a nonfiction book about a bird local to where they live and will connect with a local library to put their nonfiction bird book into circulation or on display in the children's department of the library.

Unit Overview: Throughout this unit, students will learn about the parts of birds and why they are important to a bird's survival. Students will study the lives of birds, their homes, what they eat, how they raise their young, and their life cycle. They then will write their very own nonfiction book about a native bird and connect with their local library to plan out how their book can be in circulation or displayed somewhere in the children's department of their local library.

Launch Event: Take students on a bird watching expedition with a local birding group or expert.

Module 1: Why do birds look like that?

Activities:

1. After the birding expedition, gather together to discuss what features and behaviors they noticed when observing the birds.
2. Using nonfiction books, photographs, student observations, and short video clips, research the parts of a bird and the purposes, such as the beaks, wings, feathers, talon, or different types of feet, their eyes.
3. Create a diagram and/or a 3-D model of a bird of their choice, showing each of these features and labeling them.

Module 2: What do birds do every day?

Activities:

1. Begin by researching bird habitats. Where do birds live? What are different types of bird homes? What are the different types of nests that birds make? And how do they use their home in their daily life?
2. Gathering materials that birds use to commonly build their nests at homes, have students create their own model of a specific type of a bird nest or home.

(Continued)

3. Investigate what birds eat, and how they source, capture, or hunt for their food. Show short video clips of birds that hunt or gain access to their food in different ways for students to observe.

4. Research a bird's life cycle, and how they grow and change throughout their lives. Select a specific bird to create a life cycle diagram for.

Module 3: How can I teach others about birds?

Activities:

1. Using all they have learned about birds, have students draw, color, dictate, trace, and/or write about them. Include pages for parts of birds, their habitats, the type of their home or nest, what they eat, and how they gather their food, about their young and how they're cared for, and their life cycle.

2. Plan and organize what information will go on each page and the order those pages should be in. Design and create a cover, title, about the author page, and a table of contents for their book.

3. Bind and assemble their book to be published.

4. Reach out to and meet with a local children's librarian to discuss how these nonfiction books can be a part of their library. Whether that is on display or added as a book in circulation, find a way that their writing can be seen by others in the community.

Exhibition Event: Visit the local library and take along your published bird books. Either be part of the process of cataloging it, putting it on the shelves to be in rotation, and be checked out from the library, or set up a small bird display where the books can be available for others to enjoy while they're at the library.

Learners self-selected the type of bird feeder they would create.

Adapting for smaller learning environments: For homeschooling, co-ops, and micro school settings with fewer students, individual students can write about multiple types of birds in one book, have one chapter per bird, or only write about a select bird.

My Body and Me!

Driving Question: What's inside of me and how does it work?	Public Product: Students will produce a life-sized lift the flap, layer diagram of the human body featuring the major organs and skeletal system.

Unit Overview: Throughout this unit, students will study the different body systems, including the skeletal system, muscular system, nervous system, digestive system, circulatory system, and respiratory system. As they learn about each system, they will be creating a life-size lift, the flap layered diagram of the human body. They will layer the different organs and bones so that they can be lifted up to reveal other organs and bones that are underneath. They can even write facts and information on the backside of the flap if they are ready for that level of rigor. Students will present these diagrams to their family, peers, and community members at the end of this two-month unit.

Launch Event: Invite in a local doctor, nurse, surgeon, or other medical professional to introduce students to their bodies. Have them demonstrate and allow students to experience using a stethoscope to listen to their heart and lungs, look into other people's ears and throats, and even test their reflexes.

Module 1: What do our bones do?

Activities:

1. Begin a large schema map that will be added to and utilized throughout the entire unit. Today, have students share information that they already have about the bones in their body and generate questions about the human skeleton.
2. Investigate the skeletal system through puzzles, nonfiction books, observations, short videos, and museum exhibits (virtual or in person).
3. Invite an orthopedic doctor to come and speak to the class either virtually or in person to discuss the skeletal system and its role in the human body.
4. Learn about the name, location and function of different bones in the human body.

5. Create the skeletal system layer of their large human body diagram. Begin by tracing each child on a piece of butcher paper and then providing the bone templates for them to cut out and glue as flaps onto their body in the correct locations. Add labels to important bones they learned about throughout the unit.

Module 2: How do our muscles work with our bones to make our body move?

Activities:

1. To the schema map, add knowledge they already have about their muscles and their muscular system. Generate questions about the muscular system.
2. Investigate the role of the muscular system by lifting heavy items to feel which muscles in the body are working to lift those objects.
3. Through nonfiction reading, images and photographs, diagrams, and short video clips, research and investigate how muscles are attached to the bones and how they work together to make your body move.
4. Invite a physical therapist to present to the class either virtually or in person about the role of the muscular system and its importance in the human body.
5. Create a morning movement routine to help get your muscles working each day and do them together as a class during your morning meeting.

Module 3: How does our brain tell our body what to do?

Activities:

1. Adding to the schema map, have students share what they already know about their brain and generate questions that they have about the function of their brain.
2. Investigate how their brain is the control center of their body and how it connects to our thoughts, feelings, actions, and abilities.
3. Invite a neurologist to come and discuss the brain and its role in the body with the class either virtually or in person.
4. Create a brain map, talking about the different parts of the brain and what they are responsible for.
5. Add the brain to the large human body lift-the-flap diagram underneath the skull flap that they added in module one. Write important facts about the brain on the backside of the flap and make sure to add a label.

(Continued)

Module 4: When we eat, where does our food go?
Activities:

1. Using the student schema, add what they already know about eating and their digestion and where food goes to the schema map. Have them generate questions about their digestive system or where food goes to add to their schema map.
2. Find a short video clip of the digestive system in action to observe and watch how food moves from our mouths through our body and comes out as waste.
3. Conduct an experiment and create a simulation of the digestive system in action.
4. Invite a gastroenterologist to talk about the digestive system to the class either in person or virtually to teach about how food is digested through the body and how it works with the pancreas, gallbladder, and liver to move food through the body and turn it into energy.
5. Using the digestive system and organs, write facts about each organ on the back of the flap and color and glue them into the life-size human body lift-the-flap diagram.

Module 5: Where does blood come from?
Activities:

1. Continuing on the schema map, ask students about any prior knowledge they have about their blood or blood stream. Have them generate questions about their circulatory system.
2. Through shared readings of nonfiction books and video clips, research how blood travels from the heart throughout the body.
3. Invite a phlebotomist to come and discuss with the class either virtually or in person how blood travels through the body and why it is important for the body's survival. Have them also discuss why people have their blood drawn and what they can tell from blood when they test it in a lab.
4. Add the heart to the large human body lift-the-flap diagram.

Module 6: What happens when we take a deep breath?
Activities:

1. For the final time, have students share their schema about breathing and or their lungs to the schema map, and generate questions about their respiratory system.

2. Investigate how oxygen enters the body, the function of the lungs, and how it leaves our body as carbon dioxide.
3. Conduct an experiment to simulate how our lungs work.
4. Invite a pulmonologist to either virtually or in person discuss the respiratory system and how we can keep it healthy throughout our lives.
5. Add the lungs and any other additional organs they learned about to the large human body lift-the-flap diagram.

Exhibition Event: Students will produce a life-size lift-the-flap layer diagram of the human body featuring bigger organs and skeletal system. They will present these diagrams and models to their family, school members, community members, and local medical professionals that they met throughout the unit.

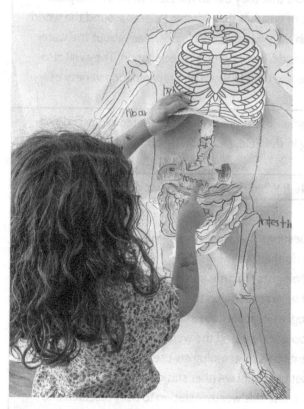

Students demonstrate their understanding of the body systems.

Creating life-size human body diagrams for our exhibition.

This unit does not need to be adapted for smaller learning groups, and it is able to be completed as is in alternative learning settings.

Jr. Meteorologists

Driving Question: How can we help others be prepared for different types of weather?	Public Product: Students will create a weather station where they can observe and chart the weather and create a weather guide where they will show what kinds of clothing and precautions to utilize for each different weather type.

Unit Overview: Throughout this unit, students will learn about the job of meteorologists and the tools that they use to measure weather. They will investigate different types of weather that different places around the world experience. They will graph daily weather conditions, learn about the water cycle, and learn what causes different types of precipitation. They will also create a guide for others to use to help them be prepared for a variety of weather events.

Launch Event: Compile some different video clips of meteorologists doing weather reports, reporting in the field, and showing different kinds of weather events.

Module 1: What do meteorologists do?

Activities:

1. Begin by generating questions that students have for meteorologists about their job and how they do their job.
2. Arrange for local meterologists to come and discuss with students how they do their job or set up an expedition to a local news station for students to see meteorologists in action and interview them about their job and how they help people understand the weather.
3. Research about different tools meteorologists use to measure weather and collect some tools to set up a mini weather station, such as a rain gauge, windsock, thermometer. Use this weather station to daily research and record the weather.
4. Began graphing the weather daily and continue to do so throughout the unit.

Module 2: What types of weather do different places experience?

Activities:

1. Create an anchor chart that outlines different types of weather, such as rain, wind, sun, thunder and lightning, snow. Have students share what they already know about these different types of weather.
2. Learn about the water cycle and create a movement series that helps students act out and name the different stages of the water cycle.
3. Create a diagram of the water cycle.
4. Discover what causes different types of precipitation, including how hot and cold air create wind and other extreme weather events.
5. Continue to research and graph the weather using your weather station.

Module 3: How can we be prepared for the weather?

Activities:

1. Create a brainstorm poster for each of the types of weather that are common in your community. Record the qualities and features of that weather on each of the posters.
2. Draw, take pictures of, or print and cut out pictures of different clothing that is appropriate for that type of weather to add to the poster.
3. Draw, take pictures of, or print and cut out pictures of different accessories, tools, and materials people may need during different weather events to add to the poster.
4. Use the posters that the students created to make their own guide in the form of a brochure, booklet, fold out, infographic, large informational poster, etc., for community members to use to be prepared for different weather events in the community.

Exhibition Event: Connect with other local schools, libraries, and community centers to distribute student guides to help others in the community be prepared for different types of weather that can occur there. Students will also continue to use their weather station so they can observe and chart the weather and report it daily over the school intercom system during announcements so other students can be prepared when they go outside.

Students graph the weather each day of the unit.

Adapting for smaller learning environments: For homeschooling, co-ops, and micro school settings with fewer students, individual students can use their weather station to report the weather to their families in order to choose what to wear for their learning time and what will be needed when they venture outside. Students will still connect with a local entity to distribute their weather preparedness guides.

I Am a Zoologist!

Driving Question: How do different animals survive and thrive?	Public Product: Students will create a "zoo" that contains their animal habitat, murals, 3-D animal sculptures, and an informational book about their animal. They will provide guided tours of the zoo using the zoom map that they create.

Unit Overview: Throughout this two-month unit, students will become experts on an animal or animals of their choice. They will learn all about annual attributes, their classification, their habitats, food, and behaviors. They will then write a nonfiction animal book, paint a mural of the animal's habitat, and create a 3-D sculpture of the animal. All of this will come together as they create a school zoo that they will provide tours of to the students and staff, their family and friends, and local community members.

Launch Event: Prior to the launch of this unit, reach out to zoos locally or across the country and request that zoom maps be sent to your classroom for an upcoming project or download and print maps from their websites. Have students investigate the maps noticing different groupings of animals, what types of animals are in similar areas of zoos, and how zoos are laid out.

Module 1: What makes my animal the same or different from other animals?

Activities:

1. Begin by going on a virtual tour of a zoo using videos from zoom websites or live feeds, or if you have a zoo or animal sanctuary local to you, go on an expedition to one of those facilities.
2. After observing a variety of animals, have students select an animal that they are most interested in becoming an expert zoologist about. If you have multiple students interested in the same animal, they can form a research team.
3. Go on an expedition to your local library to find texts on your animal and check them out to conduct research throughout this unit.

(Continued)

4. Begin by researching your animal's attributes. What makes them unique and different, what parts of their bodies are important for their survival? Create an animal diagram, showing all of these attributes and features as well as labeling them. Then turn those animal diagrams into a 3-D animal sculpture.

5. Additionally, learn about different vertebrate classifications of animals, such as mammals, fish, birds, amphibians, and reptiles. Create an anchor chart that shows all five of these classifications, and the characteristics that animals must possess to be in these classifications. Then have students draw a picture of their animal on a Post-it note and attach it to the anchor chart in the correct classification.

6. Complete the nonfiction book pages for animal attributes and classifications at the end of this module.

Module 2: Where does my animal live and how does that affect their behavior and what they eat?

Activities:

1. Using the books from the library as well as videos or live feeds from zoo, websites, read and research about what is included in your animal's habitat both in the wild and in a zoo or animal sanctuary. Make a list of what your animal will need in their habitat.

2. Learn about different animal habitats, such as deserts, grasslands, forest, jungle or rainforest, wetlands, mountains, ocean, fresh water, Arctic, Antarctic, Savannah.

3. Create an anchor chart that shows these different habitats and the characteristics of those habitats. Have students sort their animals by habitat adding a Post-it note with a picture or label of their animal to the anchor chart.

4. Group students by habitat and have them design a habitat for their animals. Then using a large piece of butcher paper, have students draw and paint a mural of the habitat which will be used as a backdrop for their zoo's presentation. They can also use leftover modeling clay from their 3-D animal sculptures to create other habitat elements that can sit in front of the mural with their animal sculptures.

5. Have students research what kind of food is available in their habitats and how they hunt or collect their food. Talk about whether different animals that have been classified in the same habitat are predators or prey in comparison to one another.

6. Complete the nonfiction book pages for animal habitats, food, and animal behavior, which can include hunting or other unique behaviors of the animal.

Module 3: How can we design a zoo to teach others all we know about our animal?

Activities:

1. Using the observations from the zoom maps from the launch event of this unit, have students begin to design and create the layout of their zoo, working together to group similar animals and habitats near each other.
2. Design and create zoom maps that will be distributed during their exhibition and zoo tours.
3. Create an animal placard for each animal sharing one way that humans can help the animals in the wild.
4. Complete any additional writing pages, such as the did you know page, table of contents, cover, and picture glossary. Assemble books to be published and available for reading at the zoo.
5. Work together to set up your zoo with the mural hanging and a small table set up in front of the mural. Students should have their placards, 3-D animal sculptures, books, and any additional habitat creations arranged on the table in front of their habitat mural.
6. Practice giving guided tours with one another or film a guided tour of the zoo for others to enjoy.

Exhibition Event: Invite other classes, families, friends, and community members to come on guided zoo tours. As people arrive at the zoo, students will greet them and present them with one of their zoo maps. They will then take them on a guided tour through each habitat telling them information about each animal. When they get to their animal that they are an expert on, they will also read them their nonfiction book.

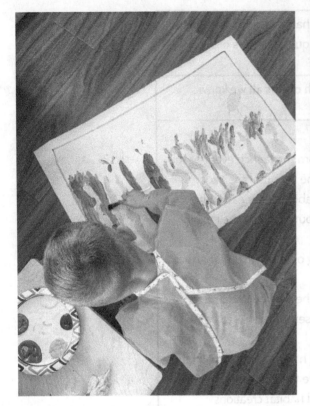

Habitat murals are painted to provide the backdrop of their animal enclosures.

Animal sculptures are crafted and painted to go in their animal enclosures.

Adapting for smaller learning environments: For homeschooling, co-ops, and micro school settings with fewer students, individual students can research multiple animals and create different habitats and animal sculptures. Students can still choose to write one full book on an animal or create one page per animal and create an animal information book. If you do not have a place to facilitate a large zoo setup or tour of the zoo, have the students film themselves presenting each animal and habitat to send to family and friends.

Blast Off!

Driving Question: What is out there in space and where do we belong in it?	Public Product: Students will host a space Expo where they will present their planet diagrams, Moon phase diagrams, constellation models, and space flip books.

Unit Overview: Throughout this unit, students will learn about the solar system including the planets and Sun and create a diagram of the planets in the relation to the Sun and Earth. They will study the phases of the Moon and chart how the Moon changes throughout the month. They will also learn about stars and space exploration and different constellations that they can see in the night sky. All of this learning will culminate in a space Expo where they will present their planet solar system diagrams, representation of the Moon phases, and a model of a constellation as well as an informational space flip book.

Launch Event: Show a video of a rocket launch to spark student excitement and interest for the unit ahead.

Module 1: What goes around the Sun?

Activities:

1. Begin by discussing what students know about planets, the solar system, and the Sun. Have students begin to think about questions that they have about our solar system.
2. Through nonfiction books, read alouds, video clips, and investigation, have students research and learn about the different planets, their characteristics and what makes them unique, their order in the solar system, etc.
3. Have students act out how planets revolve and orbit around the Sun.
4. Have students draw and paint each planet in our solar system as well as Earth's Moon, the Sun and the asteroid belt. Create labels for each. They will set these up in a large exhibition space to present at the space Expo to show the order of the planets in our solar system.
5. Complete flip book pages about the Sun and the solar system.

(Continued)

Module 2: Why does the Moon change shape?

Activities:

1. Have them act out the relationship between the Sun, Earth, and Moon using a large flashlight to show how the Earth experiences night and day and how they can see the Sun and Moon at different or the same times.
2. Have students take home a calendar with blank circles representing the Moon. Have them go outside each evening to notice the shape of the Moon and record it on their Moon phase calendar.
3. While they are charting Moon phases at home, begin studying the different Moon phases and their names in the classroom. Using clay, have students create a sculpture diagram representing the different phases of the Moon. Add labels to the Moon phases. They will present these during their space expo.
4. Complete the flip book page about the Moon phases.

Module 3: What is up in the night sky?

Activities:

1. If you are able in your community, take an expedition to a local planetarium or have a local planetarium come with their mobile planetarium to your school to teach students about the stars in the sky.
2. If you are unable to have this experience, there are plenty of online videos of planetarium presentations you can watch with your students.
3. Read about the different mythological stories behind the constellations, including their origins, and what they represent.
4. Have students select a favorite constellation and create a constellation model using toothpicks and marshmallows.
5. Set up an interview virtually with a NASA astronaut. Have students prepare questions to ask about how they became an astronaut, what they do as an astronaut, the tools that they use, and any projects they are working on.
6. Read and research about different space exploration vehicles and the different people that have explored space in the past.

Complete the space flip book pages for exploring space and additional space facts.

Exhibition Event: Students will set up a space Expo in a large exhibition space that includes their planet solar system diagrams, their 3-D Moon phase sculptures, their constellation models, and their informational space flip books. They can invite family, friends, other school members, and any community partners they met throughout the unit to come and learn about space at the Expo.

During an expedition to the science center, students got to investigate the control board inside a space shuttle.

Using pictures of the planets, students order and label them.

Adapting for smaller learning environments: For homeschooling, co-ops, and micro school settings with fewer students, individual students can choose to create and film a documentary showing the different elements that go into the space Expo exhibition in order to share their learning and materials with a wider audience even without a large exhibition space available.

Green Thumb

Driving Question: How do tiny seeds grow into large plants?	Public Product: Students will grow a plant and observe the process from seed to mature plant and record the process in a daily journal. They will create informational posters about plants and their life cycle and will beautify a local park by planting perennial flowers and shrubs native to the area.

Unit Overview: In this unit, students will learn all about plants throughout this unit including plant anatomy, what plants need to survive, and plant life cycles. They will grow a plant from seed to mature plant observing every step of the life cycle and recording them into a plant observation journal. They will research native plants to their area and select plants and shrubs that are perennial and work with the local city on how to select a park or community space that they can plant them in to beautify the space for everyone to enjoy.

Launch Event: Begin with a letter from the mayor tasking your students with learning about plants that are native to our local area and asking them to identify which ones they could plant in a local park or community space to help beautify the area for others to enjoy.

Module 1: What makes a plant grow?

Activities:

1. Bring in flowers that have very clear representation of their anatomy. Have students each take a flower and together dissect the flower separating out the different pieces, such as the roots, stem, leaves, petals, stamen, and pistol.
2. Using nonfiction texts, research and learn about the anatomy of a flower and create diagrams using the pieces of the flower they just dissected. Glue them to a piece of poster board and dictate, trace, or write labels for each of the elements.
3. Research what plants need to survive, such as sunlight, air, water, and nutrients from the soil. Discuss and/or act out how the roots bring up water and nutrients from the soil and the leaves on the plant take in sunlight and air and together they work and make food for the plant to survive.

Module 2: How does a plant grow?

Activities:

1. Using a lima bean or other fast-growing plant, wet a paper towel and place it inside of a see-through plastic bag and place two to three lima beans against the wet paper towel. Leaving the bag unzipped, tape the bag onto a window that gets plenty of sunlight.

2. In your plant observation journal record the steps for setting up your lima bean growing experiment, draw a diagram of what it looks like on day one, and write a sentence or two about your observations on the first day.

3. As the days and weeks go on, continue checking on your lima bean and recording in your journal any changes that you see. As the lima bean begins to germinate and sprout and once leaves begin to become apparent transfer the lima bean into a small cup of dirt and place on a windowsill that gets plenty of sunlight. Make sure to water regularly. Continue to journal each day that you check on your lima bean, recording any progress or changes in the bean and writing about the different stages of the life cycle that you are observing.

4. Create a diagram of the life cycle of a plant including labels and short descriptions of each stage.

Module 3: How can plants help our community?

Activities:

1. Begin to research different flowers, shrubs, grasses, or vegetation that are native to your community. Ask for donations of these plants from local businesses or school community members. You can also connect with the city department you are working with to plant the plants to see if it will provide them as well.

2. Think about the best places to plant the plants based on what you know about what plants need to survive and thrive.

3. Draw and write a proposal for the mayor about what plants you would like to plant and where you would like to plant them and why. Submit this proposal and work with the mayor to schedule a time to come and plant the plants.

Exhibition Event: Invite family members to join as you meet with the city and mayor at a local community location such as a park to plant native vegetation to beautify the park space. After the hard work is complete enjoy a picnic in the newly beautified city space.

Student flower diagram posters teach others about the inner workings of flowers.

Growing lima bean plants and observing each stage of their life cycle.

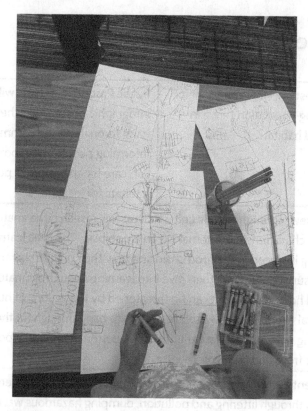

Students draw detailed flower diagrams.

Adapting for smaller learning environments: For homeschooling, co-ops, and micro school settings with fewer students, individual students can continue to choose and work with the city and invite family and friends or members of their neighborhood to help with the planting process. You can also choose to beautify the location you use for school whether that is a home or community location.

Jr. Herpetologists

Driving Question: How can we help the local frog population thrive in their natural habitat?	Public Product: Students will create infographic posters that they will hang throughout the community informing people about how they can care for and improve pond habitats for local frogs.

Unit Overview: Throughout this unit, students will research the anatomy of a frog and its characteristics that make it an amphibian. They will learn about where a frog is placed in the food chain and how their unique characteristics help them survive. They will then dive into learning about frogs' natural pond habitat and how their habitat can be threatened by the actions of humans or other natural events. They will create posters to hang throughout the community teaching others how to contribute to the bettering of natural pond habitats for frogs and their community.

Launch Event: Show students photographs of ponds that have been affected by humans through littering and pollution, dumping hazardous waste and pollutants, etc. Let students know this is where frogs must live and their habitat is being threatened by people's actions, and that it's going to be their job to help people understand how to care for pond habitats and their community.

Module 1: What makes a frog a unique amphibian?

Activities:

1. Through short video clips or nonfiction, investigate what makes a frog a frog. Learn about the features of a frog and what makes them an amphibian.
2. Draw and label a scientific diagram of a frog.
3. Create a food chain diagram or mobile that shows the predators that come before a frog and the prey that a frog consumes.
4. After learning about the predators that frogs must avoid, research and find out what frogs need to do to survive and what unique behaviors and characteristics they have that help them survive.

Module 2: How does a frog's habitat help it survive?
Activities:
1. Take an exhibition to a local pond habitat or other place in your community that frogs naturally live. If frogs do not live in your area, then you can find videos that showcase ponds and frog habitats for students to observe. 2. Discuss what a frog habitat looks like and what frogs have in their habitats and need in their habitats to survive. 3. Make a list of other animals, plants, and insects that live in or around their pond habitat. 4. Create a 3-D model or diorama of a pond habitat using recyclable materials. Add labels to show what is in the pond habitat and what is living in the pond habitat.
Module 3: How can we better the natural environment of the frogs that live in our community?
Activities:
1. Investigate ways that pond habitats and frogs are threatened or affected by humans or other natural causes. 2. Create an infographic or a flyer that tells others how they can contribute to healthy pond habitats for local frogs.
Exhibition Event: Go on an expedition throughout the community to hang up your frog pond habitat conservation flyers to help spread the information to community members about how they can be mindful of frog habitats and local ponds and ways they can contribute to keeping them healthy and thriving.

This unit does not require adaptation for alternative learning environments.

Tiny Wonders

Driving Question: Are ants friends or foes?	Public Product: Students will create, maintain, and observe an ant farm and create nonfiction books about ants to share with others.

Unit Overview: Within this unit, students will dive into a study about ants through setting up and observing an ant farm to watch ants in action. They will study the ant life cycle as well as the ways that ants move and work together as a team in their colony. They will learn about the benefits of ants in our ecosystem and their place in the food chain. They will create nonfiction ant books to share with others to help others understand that ants are friends not foes.

Launch Event: Begin by creating an either-or chart where students will take their name and place it under the statement they agree with. One side of the chart will say "I like ants," and the other side of the chart will say "I do not like ants." Prompt a discussion with students about why they chose to put their name under the statement that they did.

Module 1: What are ants and where do they live?

Activities:

1. Have students grab their magnifying glass and head out to hunt for ants in their natural environment down on the ground and use their magnifying glasses to see ants up close noticing different features, the way they move, and how they navigate the world around them.
2. Using nonfiction books and short video clips, research and begin to dispel some common myths and misconceptions that they may have about the insect.
3. Set up an ant farm so students can observe ants in action.
4. Begin to work on the ant diagram, a habitat map, an ant homes page in their nonfiction ant books they are writing throughout the unit.

Module 2: How do ants grow and change and contribute to their colonies?
Activities:

1. Through their research, study the different parts of an ant life cycle including the egg, larva, pupa, and adult stages and create a life cycle diagram.
2. Complete the ant life cycle page in their nonfiction book.
3. While observing the ants in the ant farm and out in their natural habitat, notice and record the ways that the ants move and work together. What jobs have they noticed the ants having, such as gathering food, digging the tunnels, caring for other ants, removing waste, defense, or the ones who move and bury the dead.

   * It is important to note that when you order your ant farm and your ants you will not have a queen in your ant farm colony but still discuss the role of a queen in an ant colony.
4. Work on the did you know fact page of their nonfiction book.

Module 3: What is an ant's role in our ecosystem?
Activities:

1. Do additional research about the benefits of ants in our ecosystem, such as dispersing seeds, turning over soil, adding nutrients to the soil, eating pests, or being a food source for other animals.
2. Create an ant food chain mobile that shows an ant's place in a larger food chain including what an ant eats and what eats ants.
3. Complete the ant diet page in the nonfiction book as well as the cover for the book.

Exhibition Event: As people arrive to the exhibition have them complete the same entry event that students did before starting this unit in which they will choose if they like ants or do not like ants. Then have them enter the exhibition where students will read to them their nonfiction book, show them the ant farm, explain the different roles that ants have and how they have built their underground colony, and share their ant food chain mobiles. Following the exhibition event revisit the chart from the very beginning of the launch of this unit. Have students reevaluate where they would put their name now that they know as much as they do about ants and their role in our ecosystem. Has their opinion changed, or has it stayed the same?

Connect text to hands-on research.

Investigate and observe ants in an ant farm.

Adapting for smaller learning environments: For homeschooling, co-ops, and micro school settings with fewer students, individual students can create a virtual presentation about their ants, filming their ant farm over time and doing a time lapse of their ants in the ant farm. They can also record themselves reading their book aloud and can present this digital presentation to family and friends.

Flutter Butterfly

Driving Question: How can you create an environment for butterflies to thrive?	Public Product: Students will raise butterflies, observe their life cycle changes, and plan to maintain a pollinator garden to release the butterflies into.

Unit Overview: Throughout this unit, students will learn about the life cycle of butterflies as well as their habitats and what they need to thrive in their habitat. They will also research how butterflies act as pollinators and their role in pollinating plant life. They will identify local plants that benefit butterflies in all their life stages and plant and maintain a pollinator garden to release their butterflies into.

Launch Event: When students arrive in class, have the caterpillars already ready as well as the butterfly enclosure. This will drum up excitement for students as you explain that they are going to be caring for these caterpillars as they turn into butterflies and creating a habitat for them.

Module 1: How does a caterpillar turn into a butterfly?

Activities:

1. Create a schema map for students to record what they already know about caterpillars and butterflies and generate questions that they have about them.
2. Introduce the concept of metamorphosis and the stages of a butterfly's life cycle including egg, caterpillar, chrysalis, and butterfly.
3. Create a butterfly life cycle diagram.
4. Observe the caterpillars as they create a chrysalis and emerge as a butterfly in the enclosure.
5. Have students journal about the changes that they see through drawing, dictating, or writing.

Module 2: What are the needs of caterpillars and butterflies in their habitats?

Activities:

1. Go on an expedition to a local butterfly garden or on a nature walk to observe and take notes and create drawings about butterfly habitats.
2. Through shared reading of nonfiction books and short video clips, research and record the needs of butterflies as they grow and change from egg to caterpillar to chrysalis to butterfly.

(Continued)

3. Research the food they eat, the features that help them survive their predators, and the features of their habitat and homes.
Module 3: What local flora are butterflies attracted to?
Activities: 1. Discover how butterflies act as pollinators and their role in pollinating plant life in the wild. Act out the role of butterflies as they act as pollinators.   2. Meet with the owner of a local nursery to identify local flora that will benefit the butterflies in all their life stages.   3. Collect seeds or plant starts and design and plant a pollinator garden.   4. When your butterflies are ready to be released, release them into your pollinator garden and observe and journal about the behavior you see from the butterflies in the pollinator garden.
Exhibition Event: Invite family and community members to butterfly release day to share their pollinator garden and their newly hatched butterflies.

Students demonstrate understanding in informational flip books to share with an audience.

Appropriate level research with nonfiction books, images, and manipulatives to understand butterfly life cycles.

Students create diagrams to show the parts of a butterfly.

Adapting for smaller learning environments: For homeschooling, co-ops, and micro school settings with fewer students, individual students can make a mini pollinator garden in a raised planter bed or planter pots, or connect with a local nursery to release butterflies amongst their local flora that needs pollinating.

The Earth Is Moving

Driving Question: How do plate tectonics shape our Earth, and what happens when they move?	Public Product: Students will create an Earth layer mural, build a volcano model that will erupt, and film a news segment about why volcanoes erupt.

Unit Overview: In this unit, students will explore the concepts of plate tectonics and volcanoes. Students will learn about the Earth's layers, the movement of tectonic plates, and the formation of volcanoes. They will work collaboratively to create a mural depicting the Earth's layers, build a model volcano, and produce a news segment about how volcanoes erupt. The unit culminates in an exhibition where students will display their murals, erupt their volcanoes, and play their news segments for an audience.

Launch Event: Begin by watching a video clip of a volcano erupting to pique interest and spark questions about how volcanoes are formed and why they erupt.

Module 1: What layers make up our Earth and how do they move?

Activities:

1. Begin by researching the different layers of the Earth including the crust, mantle, outer core, and inner core.
2. Using puzzles, 3-D models, images, and video clips, discover what lies beneath the Earth's surface and what makes up those different layers.
3. As a group, students will work to create a large mural that shows each of Earth's layers.
4. Research the different types of plate boundaries including convergent, divergent, and transform. On foam plates, cardboard pieces, or a large sheet of craft paper, model for students how tectonic plates move by pushing them together, pulling them apart, and sliding them past each other. Label each type of these plate boundaries.

Module 2: How are volcanoes formed?

Activities:

1. While studying the types of tectonic plates and their movement, discuss the formation of volcanoes due to the tectonic plate movement.

2. Assign students different notable volcanoes and have them research through nonfiction texts, articles, or short videos about the history of the volcano, how it was formed, and if it has erupted. If it has, what effects did its eruption have on surrounding communities?
3. Students construct their own volcano models using plastic bottles, clay or Play-Doh, baking soda, vinegar, food coloring, and trays for eruptions. Have them paint their volcanoes to look realistic.

Module 3: Why do volcanoes erupt?

Activities:

1. Now that students have researched the Earth's layers, tectonic plates and movement, and different volcanoes, we are going to study the main reasons why volcanoes erupt. Have students share their thinking about why they think volcanoes erupt to begin the investigation.
2. Study the main reasons why volcanoes erupt, including magma formation, pressure buildup, gas dissolution, crack formation, eruption, or tectonic plate movement. Look up videos of volcanoes erupting to witness these events happening with a real volcano.
3. Have students write a short script explaining how volcanoes are formed and why they erupt using their models and diagrams from Modules 1 and 2 about plate tectonic movement and volcano formation to demonstrate for their viewers.
4. Film these news segments to be presented at the exhibition event.

Exhibition Event: Students will take turns showing their news segment and, then using the baking soda and vinegar combination, have them erupt their volcano model. Students will use their layers of the Earth mural as a backdrop for their presentations.

Adapting for smaller learning environments: For homeschooling, co-ops, and micro school settings with fewer students, individual students can research a variety of different volcanoes or select one volcano to research and build their model based off that volcano. They can film both their news segment and their volcanic eruption to present to others. They can hang their mural in the background of their video news segment as well as their eruption demonstration and also use their mural to discuss the different layers of the Earth.

Dig In

Driving Question: How can we create the best soil for growing plants?	Public Product: Students will create soil composition samples where they are growing a plant, keep a plant observation journal, and create soil layer cards.

Unit Overview: In this unit, students will explore soil and its layers. Students will learn about soil composition, the importance of soil for plant growth, and how different materials affect soil quality. Students will create their own soil mixtures and plant seeds to observe how well different compositions support plant growth.

Launch Event: Set up soil exploration stations with various soil samples, such as sand, clay, and compost. Provide magnifying glasses for students to observe the soil textures and the colors closely.

Module 1: What are we standing on?

Activities:

1. Using photographs, nonfiction books, or short video clips, discuss the different layers and characteristics of soil, such as topsoil, subsoil, sand, and rocks.
2. Have students create a soil layer card where they will cut different colored paper to layer and represent the different soil layers and label each layer. Then have them brush on a thin layer of glue and sprinkle each material on the correct soil layer.
3. Head out on an expedition to collect different soil samples from different locations or have students bring different soil samples from their homes.
4. Have students observe the different types of soil from various areas and discuss the differences in color, texture, and moisture.

Module 2: Why is soil important?
Activities: 1. Students will investigate different components of soil, such as sand, silt, clay, and organic matter. Provide samples for students to touch, smell, and observe, discussing how each component contributes to the soil health. 2. Have students create different mixtures with the different soil components. Then have students pour water over their soil mixtures and observe how quickly water drains through each type of soil mixture. Have them discuss how soil composition affects water drainage. 3. After observing how different soil compositions affect water drainage, connect this information to a prior unit they have done on plant life and how plants grow and discuss the role of how soil supports plant life.
Module 3: Can plants grow here?
Activities: 1. Students will now use all they have learned about soil composition and create their own soil mixture for planting. 2. Once they have created their soil mixture, students will plant seeds in their soil mixture. 3. Students will observe and document their plant growth by regularly checking in on their plants, drawing and writing about the changes they observe over time, and caring for their plants by making sure they have water and sunlight. 4. Students will compare and contrast each group's plant growth success and discuss their soil compositions and what is making some plants grow better and some not as well based off the soil composition the plant is growing in.
Exhibition Event: Students will present their soil composition samples and their plants and explain to guests why their plant is thriving or not thriving. Students will share their observation journals with guests and teach them about the different layers and components of healthy soil using their soil layer cards.

Adapting for smaller learning environments: For homeschooling, co-ops, and micro school settings with fewer students, individual students can create a variety of soil composition mixtures to compare and contrast the different success rates of plant growth.

Scat Specialists

Driving Question: What can animal scat tell us about the animals that live around us?	Public Product: Students will create a scat identification card ring that shows different animals and features of their scat for on the trail identification of animal scat.

Unit Overview: With this unit, students will embark on an investigation of animal scat. They will research about how scat can provide valuable information about animals, their diets, and their habitats. They will create an identification ring that people can take out on the hiking trail to help them identify what animals could be around them based on scat found.

Launch Event: Take students on a nature walk to explore their natural environment and look for signs of animal scat or tracks. Have them take a clipboard and pencil and paper to observe and document any signs of scat or tracks that they find.

Module 1: What is animal scat?

Activities:

1. Set up exploration stations with pictures of various animal scat along with animal tracks and fur. Provide magnifying glasses for students to observe the images closely and discuss their findings.
2. As a class, create an anchor chart listing scat characteristics that students notice such as color, size, and shape.
3. Using modeling clay, create different models of various types of animal scat. Label with a picture and name, identifying what type of animal belongs to each scat model.

Module 2: What can we learn about animals through their scat?

Activities:

1. Research the different animals that you paired with the scat representations and create a chart that shows which of the animals eat plants, meat, or both.
2. Based on the classifications, observe the different scat models and photographs and see what similarities their scat samples have. Connect these similarities to characteristics of their scat, such as size, shape, and color.
3. Use this information about their diet and scat characteristics and compare it to the different habitats of the animals. Discuss if their habitat affects their diet, which then in turn affects the characteristics of their scat.

Module 3: How can we help others identify animals based on their scat?

Activities:

1. Students will select an animal of their choice and create a scat identification card. The card will include a picture of their chosen animal, its name, a drawing of the scat and, on the back side, will have important characteristics of the scat, what the animal eats and how that affects the scat, and what type of habitat they may find this scat in.
2. Make copies of the cards and laminate them to withstand different weather scenarios. Punch a hole in the upper left-hand corner of each laminated card and place the different cards on a jump ring.

Exhibition Event: Have students keep a copy of the scat identification ring for when they are hiking, camping, or enjoying nature with their families and friends. Also have students create enough rings that they can provide some to be available at local wildlife centers, hiking trail heads, or outdoor recreation stores for others to take on their adventures.

Adapting for smaller learning environments: For homeschooling, co-ops, and micro school settings with fewer students, individual students can create scat cards for a variety of animals rather than just making one for an individual animal.

04 Social Studies-Centered PBL Units

Social studies is all about understanding ourselves, our communities, and the world around us. Young children are naturally curious about the people they see, the places they visit, and how they fit into their surroundings. Project-Based Learning (PBL) brings these big ideas to life through hands-on, meaningful experiences that help children explore their roles as friends, family members, and community helpers. Instead of simply learning about these topics, children engage in real-world activities that build connections, encourage empathy, and foster a sense of belonging.

The following units are designed to help preschool and kindergarten learners develop foundational social studies skills, like recognizing community roles, understanding emotions, celebrating diversity, discovering the world they live in, and working together. Through hands-on activities, expedition, and expert focused units, students will learn all about themselves, their friends and family, their community, and the world they live in.

All About Me

Driving Question: Where do I fit in the world?	Public Product: Students will create a biography gallery exhibit that will include a self-portrait, bio poem, biography collage, family portrait, neighbor-hood map, and community commitment for a way to give back to their neighborhood.

Unit Overview: Throughout this unit, students will discover their own identity and what makes them different from others. They will learn about themselves, their family, family traditions, and different ways families choose to live in their local neighborhood and community. Throughout the unit, they will create different artistic expressions that represent themselves, their family, and their community, and they will all culminate in a biography, a gallery exhibit in which attendees will learn about them and their family, and their neighborhood.

Launch Event: Have a variety of posters around the room with simple questions written at the top such as, What color are your eyes? What is your favorite food? How many people are in your family? etc. Give the students markers or Post-it notes to walk throughout the room and quickly answer each question.

Module 1: What makes me unique?

Activities:

1. Gather up an essential meeting space and go on a gallery walk of the posters around the room, talking about the questions and the different answers that students recorded, making note of things that students have that are similar and things that make them different.
2. Start with visible uniqueness and what students notice upon first glance that makes them the same or different from someone else. Together, read books that talk about what makes someone unique, diversity, and how everyone's differences are accepted.
3. Provide handheld mirrors for students to look closely at the features they have that make them unique, such as skin color, eye color, hair texture and color, their gender, face shape, their height, and facial features, which includes freckles, birthmarks, adaptive tools they may use, such as cochlear implants, glasses.
4. Create a self portrait by drawing, painting, or sculpting that highlights these unique features and celebrates them.
5. Complete a bio poem that allows students to share their interests and unique characteristics that make them who they are on the inside not just what they look like on the outside.

6. Using old magazines, have students cut out pictures of things that represent them and collage them together to go with their bio poem either as a frame for the poem or in a template of a face outline.

Module 2: What makes my family unique?

Activities:

1. Read about and discuss different family structures and the different types of families that people can come from.
2. Have students talk about the family members they live with at home and family members they know who do not live in their home but still enjoy spending time with.
3. Draw, paint, color, or sculpt a family portrait that represents whom the student lives with in their home and/or additional family members who are meaningful for them that they would like to include in their portrait.
4. Read about and watch short video clips that discuss different types of homes and family dwellings. Have students create a graph as a class about the type of home that they live in, including house, trailer, apartment, condo, duplex, etc. If this is a sensitive topic for students, this can be a time when they could write their answers on a small piece of paper and place them into a box and then they can be graphed anonymously.
5. Have students create a bird's eye view map of their favorite place in their home. This could be their bedroom, the central gathering space, a play space, their backyard, etc. Discuss how to create maps using a bird's eye view technique, how to create symbols to represent elements on their map, and how to include a key and a compass rose.
6. Go around the circle and have students share about different ways that their family celebrates and remembers important events, like birthdays, holidays, religious celebrations, special traditions. Have students select their favorite family tradition and draw a picture of that tradition and dictate, trace, or write about what makes that tradition special.

Module 3: Where do I belong?

Activities:

1. Go on a walking expedition around the neighborhood that the school is located in. Talk about what can be found in the neighborhood, such as businesses, homes, parks, streets, libraries, community spaces.
2. Have students talk about what they notice in their own neighborhood. Send home a note to parents to take students on a walk one evening around their neighborhood and record different places that they have surrounding their home for students to bring back to class.

(Continued)

3. Using the same elements from the maps students made in Module 2, have students create a neighborhood or community map showing streets, important locations, their home, etc. Have them include symbols, a key, and a compass rose.

4. Discuss with students problems they notice popping up in their community that can be in the classroom, the school, on the playground, in their own home, or in their own neighborhood. Have students discuss the problem and a possible solution that they could be a part of in helping work toward solving that problem.

5. Have students paint their hands and stamp them onto a piece of paper. When they dry have students draw, dictate, trace, or write a way they could contribute something positive to their neighborhood or community that would help solve the problem that they see daily.

Exhibition Event: Students will display all of the artistic projects that they completed as a gallery wall and a larger All About Me gallery the class will present. Students can invite family, friends, school community, and other important people in their lives to come and learn all about them. Students will stand near their gallery presentation as guests rotate throughout the room, and they will tell them about themselves, their family, and how they can help the community.

Students draw and write about their favorite things.

Students draw and discuss different family makeups.

Students discuss features that make someone unique and draw a self-portrait.

Adapting for smaller learning environments: For homeschooling, co-ops, and micro school settings with fewer students, individual students can compare themselves to other members of their family, to close friends they see frequently, or even to favorite characters from books, movies, shows, etc. Students can use this project to discover more about themselves and take the community promise one step further by doing the community service project that they identified.

Can We Be Friends

Driving Question: How can we be friends with people we have never met?	Public Product: Students will create friendship bracelets to share with their classmates, as well as create a friendship pledge that they will sign.

Unit Overview: This unit is designed to be a kickoff unit at the beginning of a school year where students may or may not know one another. They will learn about themselves and their peers and understand the qualities of a good friend and develop skills to foster positive relationships. The combination of this unit will involve creating friendship bracelets to share with classmates and collaboratively signing a friendship pledge they create that reinforces the importance of kindness and respect in their interactions with one another throughout the year.

Launch Event: Begin by sitting in a friendship circle where all the children will share their name and one thing that they like: something as simple as a color, animal, or hobby.

Module 1: Who is in my class?

Activities:

1. Bring in old magazines, newspapers, toy catalogs, etc. Have students go through and cut out images of things they like or that represent them to collage on a piece of paper. Have them share these collages with their class to learn about one another.
2. Throughout this unit, play a variety of name games where students will learn and master each other's names through songs, games, fun rhymes, etc. to create a sense of community in the classroom.
3. Create a friendship web using yarn, where students will hold a piece of yarn and share something they like and then pass the yarn to another friend across the circle. Those next friends will hold on to the yarn, share something about themselves, and then toss the yarn to another friend. At the end, you will have created a friendship web that visually demonstrates connections that they can make with people in their classroom.

4. Play a game called four corners where each corner will represent a different answer to a question that you ask. For example, you could ask students which is their favorite meal of the day: breakfast, lunch, dinner, or snack time period. After pointing to each corner as you label it, count to 10 as students walk to the corner. Have them look around the group they're standing near to see who likes the same thing as them.

Module 2: What makes a good friend?

Activities:

1. Together read books that highlight diverse and positive friendships. Talk about what makes a good friend and how friends sometimes have disagreements, but they can work through them to still remain friends.
2. Practice role-playing different scenarios and act out different friendship situations that could arise in different places throughout the school day, such as in the classroom, in the hallway, at their cubbies, in the lunch room, or on the playground. Discuss how to respond to different situations in positive and friendly ways.
3. Create a friendship tree in a centralized location that students can reference in the classroom. Create a trunk with branches that is posted in the space and provide leaves to students to draw, dictate, trace, or write different qualities that make a good friend, such as kind, helpful, thoughtful, generous. Add these leaves to the friendship tree.

Module 3: How can we celebrate our friendship?

Activities:

1. Collaboratively develop a friendship pledge with the class. Discuss what promises they can make to be good friends and write those down on the poster.
2. Provide materials for students to create friendship bracelets. They can choose colors and patterns that represent themselves and their friends.

Exhibition Event: On the day of the friendship celebration, students will read together the friendship pledge they made as a class, and if they agree to the promise, they can sign their name below the pledge. Then celebrate everyone taking the friendship pledge by having them trade their friendship bracelets with their classmates.

Understanding feelings and facial expressions of our friends.

Adapting for smaller learning environments: For homeschooling, co-ops, and micro school settings with fewer students, students can use these activities and projects to deepen their relationships with siblings and family members, or turn the friendship pledge into a kindness pledge.

My Community

Driving Question: Who are the people that serve our community, and can I be one too?	Public Product: Students will create a lift-the-flap book to teach others about different community helpers and their responsibilities and will plan and carry out a service project for a local community organization.

Unit Overview: Throughout this unit, students will learn about different jobs that people do in their community, the tools that they use to do their jobs, and how their jobs help others. They will then teach others about these jobs by creating a lift-the-flap book. They will also partner with a community organization to find out how they can be a community helper and do a service project that can benefit that organization.

Launch Event: Have students share what they want to be when they grow up and create a list of their answers.

Module 1: Who are the helpers?

Activities:

1. Using the list that students created of job ideas for what they want to be when they grow up, have students write invitations for individuals that do those jobs, inviting them to the class to share about their job. Mail out or deliver these letters inviting local community members to come and present to the class.
2. Have a variety of community members come to the class to discuss their jobs, how they help others in the community, the tools they use to do their job, and what someone has to do to obtain that job.
3. Have students read books about the job prior to their arrival and generate questions to ask the presenter. Following the visit have students create thank you cards to send to the community helper.

Module 2: Do others know the helpers?

Activities:

1. As you meet all the community helpers, create an anchor chart that shows the community helpers' title, where they work, what they do during their work day, whom they help by doing their work, special tools they might need for their job, and what kind of learning they have to do to be able to have this job.

(Continued)

2. Use the information from this chart to create a book page for each of the community helpers. Have students draw a picture of the community helper and glue it along the top of the background page. Then lift up the community helper and write below it a summary of this information.
3. Once all pages are complete, create a cover and bind together to publish a lift-the-flap book all about local community helpers to have in the classroom or school library.

Module 3: How can I be a helper?

Activities:

1. Reach out to a variety of community organizations and have students select one that they would like to partner with or have a personal interest in. This could even be an organization that one of your community helpers is connected with.
2. Have students interview the organization or workplace to see if they have any specific needs. Have students brainstorm a service project that they can plan and execute independently or involve their friends and families to help contribute to the needs of this organization.

Exhibition Event: Carry out the service project that the students designed. Following the service project's completion have students reflect about how it felt to help others in their community and have them revisit the list from the beginning of the unit about what they wanted to be when they grow up and see if that is still what they would like to be or if they met someone who has a job that seemed even more exciting to them.

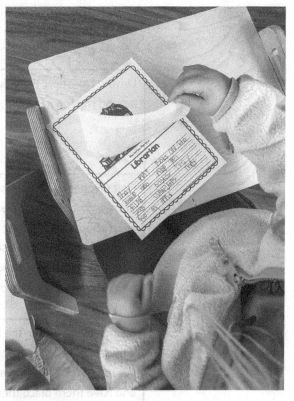

A local hairstylist visited our class to teach about her job.

Students write about librarians and how they help our community.

Adapting for smaller learning environments: For homeschooling, co-ops, and micro school settings with fewer students, if students cannot invite these individuals into their homes, students can go on many expeditions to different workplaces to meet with, interact with, and interview different community helpers. There are also a lot of ways to virtually connect with different professionals and many short video clips that show what different community helpers do daily. They can also pick a community service project that has a smaller scale, or they can invite family and friends and their neighborhood community members to join in on their service project.

From Here to There

Driving Question: How do people get around my town?	Public Product: Students will produce a picture book that shows photographs that they took of vehicles and forms of transportation in their community.

Unit Overview: Throughout this unit, students will learn about different types of transportation that people use to get from here to there. They will also learn about the different vehicles people use and the jobs that those vehicles are used for. They will also go on weekly walks where they will snap photos of different forms of transportation and vehicles that they see in their community to create their very own photographic nonfiction picture book of transportation.

Launch Event: Along the bottom of a piece of chart paper, write or put pictures of different types of transportation that students might have used to get to school. Give students a sticker or a Post-it note with their name on it and have them place their sticker above the mode of transportation they used to create a graph. Talk about the results of the survey and what type of transportation was the most or least popular for getting kids to school.

Module 1: How do people travel?

Activities:
1. Begin with a schema map asking students what they already know about different vehicles and transportation. List the names of different types of transportation and vehicles that they are already familiar with.
2. Using nonfiction books, photographs, and short video clips, learn about different types of vehicles that people use to travel by air, land, and sea.
3. Compare and contrast different forms of transportation identifying features making them unique or that they have in common with other vehicles both in their transportation category and in others.
4. Create a poster that shows air, land, and sea and have a variety of vehicle pictures printed off. Have students work together to sort and glue the pictures into the correct transportation category.

Module 2: What jobs do vehicles have?
Activities:
1. Using nonfiction books, photographs, and short video clips, research different types of vehicles and the job that they do. Focus on types of vehicles that help people, such as first responder vehicles, farming vehicles, construction vehicles, commuting vehicles, or vehicles used for distance traveling.   2. Investigate the different community members that might drive, fly, conduct, etc. the vehicles that help people in their community.
Module 3: What transportation do I see in my community?
Activities:
1. Throughout the unit, schedule weekly walks as a class or challenge their family to go on weekly walks, and using a camera or a tablet, snap photos of different forms of transportation or vehicles that they see on their walk in their community.   2. Connect with different community helpers and set up tours of their vehicles, such as fire trucks, police cars, farm tractors, mail delivery trucks, delivery drivers. Make sure to snap photos of those vehicles.   3. Take time to print each of the pictures and glue them each to their own page for a transportation book that they can make available in their classroom and school library. Have students dictate, trace, or write the label for each of the transportation vehicles as well. If they are also independent writers, they can write a sentence about each vehicle, the type of transportation they provide, and how they help the community.
Exhibition Event: Students can share their books with friends and family in the school community by making sure a copy is available in the classroom library and the school library. They can also provide copies of the page that they made about the community helper vehicles that they were given tours of to the community helper.

Sorting transportation by air, land, and sea.

Coloring different types of transportation for our transportation books.

Adapting for smaller learning environments: For homeschooling, co-ops, and micro school settings with fewer students, individual students can connect with their local library, a local preschool, or a local kindergarten to find a library that would like a donation of their transportation vehicle book.

Welcome to Our School

Driving Question: How can we help new students and families feel welcome and informed about our school?	Public Product: Students will create a video showcasing a guided tour of their school. It will include short clips of staff interviews, highlights of important locations throughout the school and will be presented during back to school nights and made available on the school's website.

Unit Overview: Throughout this unit, students will learn about various school locations, important staff members, and resources available to students and families when they attend the school. Students will create a detailed school map, compile a directory of school staff with short biographies, and film a guided tour of the school that will be shown during open house nights and be available on the school website.

Launch Event: Begin this unit with a school scavenger hunt. Prepare a simple scavenger hunt list that includes common areas of the school, such as the library, cafeteria, gym, playground and have students explore these places and take notes about what they discovered and how these areas are helpful to the school community.

Module 1: What is inside our school?

Activities:

1. Begin by taking a guided walk around the school with the students, allowing them to take pictures of various locations that can later be used on their school maps and in their video.
2. Work together as a group to create a bird's eye view school map that includes important locations like classrooms, the library, the playground, etc.
3. After identifying key areas in the school, students will create labels for each location, and these labels will be added to the school map. They can also print off photographs as one-inch squares to attach to their map of key areas in the school building.

(Continued)

Module 2: Who are the important people in our school?

Activities:

1. As a group, generate questions that students would want to ask important staff members of the school community. Compile these questions into a one-page interview sheet.
2. Schedule times for important staff members to come to the classroom or for students to go and visit them to conduct the interviews based off the interview sheets that they created. Have students also snap a photograph of the staff member.
3. Compile the information gathered from interviews to create a short biography of those staff members that includes their photograph, name, and a few sentences about them and what they do in the school.
4. Add these biographies to the school website or create a small placard for each of the staff members to put outside of their office or classroom for students and families to read about when they come to the school.

Module 3: What do new families need to know when they come to our school?

Activities:

1. Create small groups of students and assign each group to an important area of the school. Have them identify key features of that area, what students will do or how they will use that area of the school, and why it is important. They can also highlight important rules to remember when they are in that area of the school. You can also assign some groups of students to interview important staff members during the tour such as the principal, secretary, librarian, school resource officer, playground monitor, etc.
2. Have students create a simple script that they will use when filming their short clip for the video tour.
3. Set aside time for students to rehearse and practice their scripts and for them to decide what features they want to point to and highlight during their film segment. Have students use tablets to record one another giving their tour of the section of the school they were assigned. Encourage them to be enthusiastic and welcoming and remind them that this will be a video that new families and students will see to introduce them to the school and the school community.
4. Add together the different clips in an order that the class decides on and preview the video as a group.

Exhibition Event: Add this welcome tour video to your school's website for prospective families to view when learning more about the school. Also make the video available for any back to school or open house nights for new families that are joining the school community.

Adapting for smaller learning environments: For homeschooling, co-ops, and micro school settings with fewer students, individual students can provide tours of their learning space. They could highlight areas, such as a reading corner, library, independent workspaces, gathering spaces, art stations.

A Kid's Guide to the City

Driving Question: What are the most fun and kid friendly places in our city?	Public Product: Students will create a map/guide to kid friendly places to visit in their city.

Unit Overview: In this unit, students will learn about their local community and collaborate to create a colorful map showcasing locations that are kid friendly. They will publish their maps and guides and distribute them to their local City Hall so visitors to their community can find fun and kid friendly things to do while they are in town.

Launch Event: Have students do a show and tell about their favorite thing to do in their city. They can bring photos or small trinkets that represent these locations.

Module 1: What is there to do in our city?

Activities:

1. Take a walk around the neighborhood to observe local landmarks and kid-friendly places. Encourage students to take let's draw pictures of the places that they notice.
2. Invite community members, such as local librarians, park rangers, or business owners to talk about the places in the city that are fun for kids. Have students ask questions about each location and potentially schedule a time to visit their establishment.
3. Help students research different kid-friendly spaces in their community through using the Yellow Pages, Google map searches, and sites like TripAdvisor, etc.

Module 2: What makes these places kid friendly?

Activities:

1. Prior to this module collect books and brochures and have websites open on tablets about local attractions. Have students cycle through different stations where they can work in pairs or small groups to gather information about the different kid-friendly spaces in the community.

2. As a group, discuss the characteristics that make a place kid friendly, such as fun activities, safety, accessibility, price. Have students create a list of features they find most important that they would want to include in their map or guide when highlighting an establishment.

3. Plan and go on simple field trips to a few local attractions, such as parks, museums, zoos. Students can explore these places and gather information and experiences to include in their maps and guides. Have students compare these locations against the characteristic list that they made prior.

Module 3: How can we help other families discover these activities?

Activities:

1. Have students study different city maps to help them decide on how they would like to lay out their kid-friendly city map guide. Have them decide on their color scheme, different symbols that they want to use to represent types of locations, and how they will label these locations.

2. Make a list of all the locations students visited, learned about, or researched. Give each student three dot stickers to vote on their top three favorite attractions. Select the most popular based on those votes to include in their city map and guide.

3. Assign small groups of students to different locations and have them write a simple description of two to three sentences for each location that will be included on the map explaining why it's fun for kids, highlighting important features of this location that could help families understand if it would be a great place for their family to visit. Work together to create a bird's eye view map of their city and type up and add their descriptions to the map. Have students add illustrations, stickers, or other embellishments to their maps to make them visually appealing to families that will use the maps.

Exhibition Event: Students will make multiple copies of their guides to the city and take an expedition to City Hall or their city's visitor center to add their maps to their tourism displays for visiting families to use to find kid-friendly activities to do while they visit the city.

Students visit a local farm to write a review and recommendation.

Adapting for smaller learning environments: For homeschooling, co-ops, and micro school settings with fewer students, individual students will write the descriptions for each of the locations they want to include in their map or guide. They will type up and create the map independently and make portable copies to partner with their local City Hall or visitor center to distribute the maps to visiting families.

Mountains and Valleys, Rivers and Lakes

Driving Question: How can we teach others about the landforms that shape our Earth?	Public Product: Students will create 3-D models and watercolor paintings of landforms.

Unit Overview: Throughout this unit, students will explore various landforms and bodies of water. They will learn to identify different landforms and understand their characteristics and how they were formed. Students will create 3-D models of landforms found in the real world and pair them with photographs and watercolor paintings of the landforms.

Launch Event: Begin by showing students pictures of places they like to explore, such as the beach, hiking, fishing on a river, skiing on a mountain. Have them notice and wonder about the things they see in the setting. Record their thinking and questions on Post-it notes and attach them to the pictures.

Module 1: What is a landform?

Activities:

1. Introduce common landforms that they see daily in their own community or in their reading. Explore different landforms in nonfiction and even fictional texts. Begin an interactive anchor chart where you'll post photographs of landforms and have students trace or write the label for the name of the landform.
2. Using landform picture cards and labels, have students practice naming, labeling, and matching landforms.
3. As a class, search through nature magazines and publications and cut out pictures of different landforms and glue them to the poster to show different representations of landforms.

Module 2: How do landforms form?

Activities:

1. Using a large tub or tray, sand, and water, conduct an experiment where water will travel through the sand in different ways to model the formation of landforms and the types of bodies of water that are created at the same time.
2. Set up a sensory bin in the classroom with sand, rocks, water, etc., for students to explore and create different landforms and bodies of water.
3. Using clay, students will create models of different landforms and paint them to represent a landform they have observed throughout research.

(Continued)

Module 3: What landforms are in our community?

Activities:

1. Go on an expedition to a local park, nature reserve, hiking trail, etc., to explore landforms and bodies of water in the real world.
2. Take photographs of each of the landforms and bodies of water observed.
3. Using watercolor paper and paint, students will paint a watercolor representation of the landform they photographed and write a label and short sentence/description of the landform.

Exhibition Event: Students will present their 3-D landform sculptures, watercolor paintings, and classroom poster to their classmates, school community, family, friends, and community members. They can also have mini sensory bins set up to demonstrate their understanding of landform creation.

Adapting for smaller learning environments: For homeschooling, co-ops, and micro school settings with fewer students, individual students can select to do a 3-D model of multiple landforms or a mass of landforms together. They can also choose to make individual small book pages rather than a large poster of each of the landforms.

Did You See That?

Driving Question: What landmarks in our city are important for others to learn about?	Public Product: Students will create a city guidebook that will teach others about important landmarks and be available at their local City Hall and/ or museum.

Unit Overview: Throughout this unit, students will explore major landmarks throughout their city. Through meeting with local experts, heading out on expeditions, and conducting interviews, students will create a guidebook that will highlight the unique features and significance of a variety of landmarks in their community.

Launch Event: Present a prerecorded video from a local historian, member of city council, etc., introducing themselves to the students and tasking them with creating a guidebook of their community's local landmarks to share with visitors and residents of the city.

Module 1: What is a landmark?

Activities:

1. Introduce the concepts of landmarks by looking at books and pictures of famous landmarks they may be familiar with such as: Statue of Liberty, Pyramids, Big Ben, Golden Gate Bridge, Mt. Rushmore, etc.
2. Have students brainstorm different landmarks that they are already familiar with in their community.
3. Watch a tourism video for your city and note any landmarks they spotted during the video.
4. Create a list of landmarks they want to learn more about in their community.

Module 2: Let's explore our city!

Activities:

1. Set up a variety of expeditions to local landmarks in your community. When visiting the landmarks, make sure to have the students photograph the landmark, explore it, and make notes about important features of the landmark.
2. Have students record voice memos about what they enjoyed about visiting the landmark and why others might want to visit, also.

(Continued)

3. Have students compile their pictures and observations into individual landmark posters in the classroom to use for creating their guide later on.

Module 3: Who can teach us more?

Activities:

1. Invite in or go visit local City Hall or city council. Have students ask questions about the landmarks they visited and learn more about the significance of the landmark in the community.
2. Invite in or go visit local historian who can give students information about why the landmark was erected, the history of it, details about how it was built, etc.
3. Have students add this new learning to their landmark posters.
4. Assign groups of students to the different landmarks to have them create a one-page informational sheet for their local landmark. They should include the best photograph they have for it, facts and information about it, history, and their "reviews" as quotes at the bottom of the page. Compile into a book and have students design covers for them.

Exhibition Event: Have students deliver their guidebooks (make multiple copies) to local museums, visitor centers, library, City Hall, and other community places where their guidebooks can be shared with the community and tourists.

Adapting for smaller learning environments: For homeschooling, co-ops, and micro school settings with fewer students, individual students can create the various pages, rather than working in groups. They may choose to do half-sheet smaller blurbs about the landmarks rather than a full page for each. They could also record short video clips of their reviews to share with the city to share on their local websites.

This Is How We Do It

Driving Question: How can we honor and share our family's culture and traditions with our community?	Public Product: Students will hold a cultural fair where they will each have a trifold poster that shares about their family, traditions, food, and ancestry. They will also create a family crest for their poster.

Unit Overview: Throughout this unit, students will explore and celebrate their unique cultural heritage. They will research about their family's traditions, foods, languages, and ancestral origins. Students will create a trifold presentation board to showcase their learning at a class cultural fair. In addition, they will create a family crest that will be in the center of their board.

Launch Event: Play the "step forward if" game where you will have all students line up on a line. Then call out things that families may have in common, such as holidays they celebrate, foods they may enjoy, places they may be from, languages spoken. Have students step forward if the things are true about their family, or have them stay on the line if not true about their family.

Module 1: How does my culture help my family create traditions?

Activities:

1. Begin by diving into what culture is through reading stories, using picture books that highlight different cultures, etc.
2. Ask students to bring in pictures of things that represent their family's culture, such as holiday celebrations, foods, clothing, regalia, decorations. Share them with one another to talk about similarities and differences.
3. Research cultural symbols, such as flags, clothing, jewelry, dishes, art that represent the cultures in the classroom. Print and cut them out and make a class collage of the various cultures.
4. Brainstorm interview questions students can ask their parents or family about their cultural background, traditions, favorite foods, etc.
5. Conduct family interviews and bring back the answers to share with the group.
6. Create a classroom map that shows where students or their ancestors are from. Use stickers to mark where they are from and attach a string to a picture of the student.

(Continued)

Module 2: Does my culture affect the food I eat and the language I speak?

Activities:

1. Using information from students' family interviews, make a list of the different languages spoken by the families or cultures represented in the class. Make a list of common phrases/greetings/words that students could learn from each language, such as hello, goodbye, thank you, please.
2. Reach out to families to send in a small sample of foods, snacks, drinks, tastes, etc., that connect their family to their cultural heritage. Have a food tasting day where students can sample small pieces of food/drink from their classmate's cultures.
3. Add to the classroom map showing photos of the foods, flags, language, and cultural dress for each of the places students are from.
4. Invite family members who are interested and/or able to come in and share about their culture with the class.

Module 3: How can I share what is important to my family's culture?

Activities:

1. Share photos of different family crests and talk about the symbolism and representation of their culture on the crest.
2. Provide students with a crest template to design and create their own family crest. Glue this to the center of their trifold presentation board.
3. Students will use photographs or drawings to create their trifold presentation that shares their country of origin, the language, a few common phrases they can share, cultural dress/regalia, food, flag, and a country map.
4. Have students dictate, trace, or write a few sentences about their culture they would like to share.

Exhibition Event: Students will set up their presentation boards around a large space. Families, friends, school community, and community members will circulate throughout the room to stop and learn from each student about their culture and history.

Adapting for smaller learning environments: For homeschooling, co-ops, and micro school settings with fewer students, individual students can research their family culture and present their crest and trifold to their family and friends. Students could also try recreating a dish to share. Students could also choose to research cultures from both sides of their family if they differ from one another and share about those similarities and differences during their presentation.

Around the World in 80 Days

Driving Question: How can we showcase unique characteristics of each continent to entice people to visit?	Public Product: Students will create a commercial highlighting the unique features of their selected continent, inviting others to visit it.

Unit Overview: In this unit, students will research and learn about the seven different continents including elements, such as habitats, animal life, landscape, famous landmarks, people groups. Students will then select their favorite continent and work with a team to film a commercial about the continent, encouraging others to go visit it.

Launch Event: Play a video clip of each continent or a video about the different continents on Earth for students to begin to understand the vast amount of land on our planet and that each land mass has a name.

Module 1: What makes up a continent?

Activities:

1. Begin by understanding the concept of a continent and being able to recognize, identify, and name them on a map. Include continent puzzles, matching games, vocabulary cards, etc.
2. Set up stations for each continent that include books, photographs, video clips, artifacts, money, flags, etc., that represent the continent. Allow students to rotate through the stations to begin to make connections to different continents and their unique features.
3. Identify different habitats of each continent. Make a poster for each continent and record the different habitats found on the continent and add photographs/images of those habitats.
4. Learn about animals that are unique to those habitats on that continent. Add these animals and their pictures to the posters for each continent.
5. Read about, study images, and watch video tours of famous landmarks (natural or man-made) from each continent. Add photographs and labels of these to your posters.
6. Take time to research the different native people groups and cultures that are a part of each continent. Add different flags, cultural people groups, unique dress, foods, languages, etc., to the continent's poster.

(Continued)

Module 2: What makes each continent unique?

Activities:

1. North American Exploration: Dive deep into investigating the geography, wildlife, and major cultural and indigenous groups of North America. Discuss the different countries that make up North America, their similarities and differences from one another, the languages spoken, currency used, etc.

2. South American Exploration: Discover the rainforests, mountains, indigenous people groups, and fascinating wildlife of the South American continent. Discuss the different countries that make up South America, their similarities and differences from one another, the languages spoken, currency used, etc.

3. European Exploration: Explore the many countries that make up Europe, the different traditions celebrated by the people of those countries, the many famous landmarks, the variety of currencies and languages used throughout Europe, etc.

4. African Exploration: Research the diverse landscapes across Africa, the unique wildlife, and the variety of cultures of the indigenous people groups that reside in Africa. Discuss the different countries that make up Africa, their similarities and differences from one another, the languages spoken, currency used, etc.

5. Asian Exploration: Investigate the different cultures, landscapes, and famous landmarks in Asia. Discuss the different countries that make up Asia, their similarities and differences from one another, the languages spoken, currency used, etc.

6. Australian Exploration: Discover the exciting wildlife and landscapes of Australia. Discuss the different states and territories that make up Australia, their similarities and differences from one another, the languages spoken, currency used, etc.

7. Antarctic Exploration: Learn about the environments and wildlife of Antarctica and the way scientists use Antarctica to study. Discuss the importance of polar habitats and our effects on them.

Module 3: How can I convince others to visit a continent?

Activities:

1. Have students select which continent is their favorite and the one they would like to focus on for their commercial. Team students up to work together on their commercial.
2. Meet in teams to talk about what they want the commercial to focus on, their favorite parts of the continent, what they want to share with viewers, etc.
3. Write short sentences students will want to say on camera that share about the highlights of the continent they are focused on.
4. Create a storyboard where students will draw out and plan the different scenes of their commercial.
5. Create and gather the materials needed for the commercial, such as costumes/outfits, photographs, drawings, artifacts.
6. Using a tablet or camera, have students work with their teams to film their commercials.

Exhibition Event: Students will invite classmates, school community, friends, and family to the commercial premier. Play each commercial and then have attendees write feedback about what continent they would want to visit and why. After the premier, meet in teams and review the feedback from the audience.

Adapting for smaller learning environments: For homeschooling, co-ops, and micro school settings with fewer students, individual students can select an individual continent and create their commercial to share virtually with friends and family. They could also choose to do a commercial for each continent and then have viewers vote for which continent they would want to visit after viewing all seven clips.

05 ELA-Centered PBL Units

Language and literacy are all about communication, expressing ideas, sharing stories, and making sense of the world through words. Young children are natural storytellers, eager to describe their experiences, ask questions, and engage with books, songs, and conversations. Project-Based Learning (PBL) brings these skills to life through hands-on, meaningful experiences that help children develop a love for language while building confidence in their ability to read, write, listen, and speak. Instead of simply practicing letters and sounds in isolation, children engage in real-world activities that make literacy fun, interactive, and purposeful.

The following units are designed to help preschool and kindergarten learners build foundational literacy skills, like recognizing letters and sounds, developing vocabulary, telling stories, and understanding the power of communication. Through hands-on, inquiry-driven projects, students will explore the magic of books, the joy of storytelling, the importance of listening and speaking, and the many ways we use language every day.

I am an Author

Driving Question: How can we use different versions of the same classic tale to guide us in writing our own version?	Public Product: Students will publish an original storybook inspired by a classic tale.

Unit Overview: Throughout this unit, students will read, compare, and contrast multiple versions of a popular classic tale. They will learn about the elements of a fictional story and plan out and write their own version of a classic storybook.

Launch Event: To kick off this unit, begin by asking students about their favorite fairy tales and fables. Generate a list together of these different books.

Module 1: How are these stories the same and different?

Activities:

1. Select a popular storybook, such as The Gingerbread Man, Little Red Riding Hood, Jack and the Beanstalk. Begin by reading the original version to the class.
2. On a large anchor chart, create a table that has columns for the title, characters, setting, problem, and solution. Start by recording the information from this original story onto the chart.
3. Throughout the first week or two, continue reading different retellings of the same story. As you read them, record the information on the chart. Record similarities to the original in green and differences in red so students can see the comparison.
4. Introduce the Venn Diagram and have students compare some of the retellings to the original version of the story or to one another.

Module 2: What if I wanted to write my own version?

Activities:

1. Discuss the elements of a story: characters (protagonist and antagonist), main vs. secondary characters, what characters can be in a fiction story (people, mythical creatures, animals, objects, etc.), setting, problem, and solution.
2. Using a story map graphic organizer, have students identify the characters they want in their retelling: which will stay the same, and what characters will be unique to their story.

3. Identify possible settings that could appear throughout the book. Record them on the story map.
4. Have students use the same problem from the original story but add their own spin to it to make it unique to their characters and settings.
5. Plan the ending to their story. Will it be a happy ending? Will it differ from the original or be similar?

Module 3: How do I write a storybook?

Activities:

1. Plan and write the hook of the story. How will you catch the reader's attention right from the beginning. Create a chart with the different types of hooks writers use to catch the attention of their readers.
2. Introduce the concept of how words convey the passage of time. Identify different words or phrases that relate to the beginning of a story, moving the story along, and wrapping a story up. Encourage students to use these words and phrases as they move through the events of their story.
3. Talk about important writing elements, such as capitalization rules, spaces between words, and appropriate punctuation.
4. Add detailed illustrations to each page that help tell the story and relate to the words written on the page.
5. Create a cover page and bind the book together.

Exhibition Event: Students will read their storybooks aloud to small groups or friends and family, school community, or peers.

Students assemble their writing to publish their stories.

Provide supports and tools for students to be successful throughout the writing process.

No adaptations necessary for alternative learning environments.

Rhyme Time

Driving Question: How can we make rhyming fun for other learners?	Public Product: Students will work together to create a classroom rhyming book to be enjoyed for future students in the class.

Unit Overview: Throughout this unit, students will learn about rhyming and word families and use their phonics skills to write a class rhyming book that will be used by future classes to learn about and recognize rhyme.

Launch Event: Read aloud a few popular rhyming books.

Module 1: Can you hear the rhyme?

Activities:

1. Read aloud rhyming books throughout the unit. As you read, have students give you a symbol for when they hear rhyming words. Stop and ask them to share the rhymes they hear as you read.
2. Give students different picture cards that have a rhyming match with another student's card. Have students find their match throughout the group and share their rhyming pair with the class.
3. Set up rhyming centers and have students rotate through different rhyming activities, such as rhyming match puzzles, rhyming memory games with a small group, rhyming sorts.
4. Play "rhyme or no rhyme" where you read off a pair of words and have students give you a thumbs up if they rhyme or a thumbs down if they don't rhyme.

Module 2: Can you read the rhyme?

Activities:

1. Using onset and rime, introduce consonant-vowel-consonant (CVC) word families that are fairly common for students to be able to hear and identify, such as -at, -ap, -et, -en, -it, -ig, -ot, -og, -un, -up.
2. Practice blending words using onset and rime by showing a consonant card and then the word family ending and having students segment and blend the word: /c/ /at/ = cat.

(Continued)

3. Provide word chains or word family words and have students practice reading the chain of rhyming words: cat, bat, hat, fat, mat, rat, sat.
4. Have students sort picture cards into word family groups.
5. Have students read decodable texts and record words onto chart paper for each word family.

Module 3: Can you make a rhyme?

Activities:

1. Write a word family ending on the board or a piece of chart paper. Have students generate as many rhyming words as they can (one or multiple syllable words). Record the words they generate.
2. Have students look at the words on their list and brainstorm phrases and short stories that could use a variety of the words generated, for example, "The fat cat sat on a mat looking for a rat."
3. Have students write a sentence or series of sentences using as many rhyming words as they can from the list and illustrate a picture to go with it.
4. Repeat this with multiple different rhyming word families.
5. Have students compile their rhyming poems into an anthology book and create a cover.

Exhibition Event: Students will each get to keep a copy of their class book, as well as place a copy in the classroom and/or school library for future students to read and enjoy.

Adapting for smaller learning environments: For homeschooling, co-ops, and micro school settings with fewer students, individual students can create their rhyming book and connect with a local preschool or childcare center to gift their rhyming book.

Alphabet Master

Driving Question: How can we help other kids learn their ABCs?	Public Product: Students will create an alphabet game that they will teach to their classmates to help them practice their ABCs.

Unit Overview: Students will use their knowledge of letter names, sounds, and symbols to design and create their very own alphabet game that they will teach to their peers. It will end with a game day where everyone will rotate through the different games to try them out.

Launch Event: Set out common games that students likely know how to play, such as Candy Land, Chutes and Ladders, Connect 4, Guess Who, Go Fish, Memory Games. Have a game party where they get to play the different games.

Module 1: Do you know your ABCs?

Activities:

1. Practice identifying letter names by using flash cards to identify a letter and call out the name. You can also make a letter sound and have students identify the name of the letter that matches that sound.
2. Practice recalling letter sounds sorting pictures or objects by their beginning sound and matching them to the letter symbol that represents that sound.
3. Practice identifying uppercase and lowercase letters by matching magnetic letters or flash cards into pairs.
4. Set out letter stations that include activities, such as alphabet puzzles, letter matching, letter sound sorts to have students practice and review their phonics skills.

Module 2: What makes a good game?

Activities:

1. Circling back to the launch activity, ask students to tell you which games they enjoyed most.

(Continued)

2. Once you have this list, ask students to identify why they liked these games most. Have them give more than just "it was fun." Instead, have them really think about what made the game fun. Was it how many people could play? Did they like that it was a card game or board game? Was it fast paced and exciting? Make a list of the qualities of the games.
3. Create an anchor chart of the different categories of games they have played, such as card game, memory game, matching game, board game. Draw a picture or print off and glue a picture as an example for each type of game. Write the different features of those games, such as uses a dice, spinner, deck of cards, game pieces, etc. that make that game style unique.

Module 3: How can we turn our ABCs into a game?

Activities:

1. Have students select the type of game they would like to make. You can also put them in pairs or small groups with peers who are interested in making the same style of game.
2. Have them meet and discuss/select the focus of their ABC game. Will they work on letter names, letter sounds, letter symbols, writing letters, match-ing uppercase and lowercase, etc.
3. Have them begin to design and plan out the play of the game. What is the goal of the game, what types of moves/actions will players take through-out the game, what materials do they need to play, such as game pieces, a board, cards, dice?
4. Have students draw plans for their game pieces. What will the board look like, what design will be on cards, etc.
5. Begin to create final draft versions of the games/pieces. Game boards can be made on cardboard, cereal boxes, thick tagboard, etc. Precut cards from card stock. Provide spinner templates and dice patterns.
6. Have students draw, dictate, or write their game rules. For non-writers, a talk to text setup may be best.
7. Practice playing the game multiple times and make changes updates as needed.
8. Partner with another team to test out one another's games and provide feedback for finishing touches.

Exhibition Event: Students will have their games set up for other students and classes to rotate around and play.

Students can identify letters in different fonts.

Matching uppercase and lowercase letters and identifying their phonetic sound.

Adapting for smaller learning environments: For homeschooling, co-ops, and micro school settings with fewer students, individual students can create a game and invite over family or friends with same age or a bit younger child that can enjoy playing the game or games with them.

Jr. Critics

Driving Question: How can we help others discover and love new books?	Public Product: Students will create a public display of children's book reviews that allow other kids to learn about the books and why they should read them.

Unit Overview: Throughout this unit, students will learn about book publishing, the different roles of individuals involved in publishing a book, and the importance of audience reviews and feedback in the promotion of a book. Students will select favorite read aloud books and create reviews for them that others will be able to read or listen to help them select a book to read or check out next. They will partner with a local public or school library to share their book reviews.

Launch Event: Display a popular read aloud book that the class has enjoyed this year. Ask students to draw, dictate, or write on a Post-it note about their favorite part about the book. Have them share their thoughts and stick it on the cover of the book.

Module 1: How are books made and published?

Activities:

1. Gather a variety of book styles, board books, paperback, hard cover, dust jackets, novels, etc. and talk about the various features of the books. Compare and contrast their similarities and differences based on their appearance, binding, size, etc.
2. Watch a video clip about how a book is bound/made and how books are cared for.
3. Research roles of individuals involved in the making of a book, such as an author, illustrator, researcher, agent, editor, publisher, and more.
4. Coordinate an expedition to your local library to learn about the different jobs at the library, how books move through the library, different programs libraries offer and get a tour of the behind the scenes areas of the library.

Module 2: Does my voice matter?

Activities:

1. Throughout the unit, continue to read a variety of fiction and nonfiction books of high interest topics and themes for your students.

2. Have the students select their favorite or most enjoyed book and complete a story elements graphic organizer, including the characters, setting, problem and solution for a fictional book or a main idea and supporting details page for a nonfiction book.
3. Have students write and draw about their favorite parts of the book. What makes them like it so much and what might others also like about it?
4. Have students write or dictate one to three sentences about what would excite a reader about reading this book.
5. Set the books up with their sentence reviews in the classroom for peers to read and explore the favorite books their classmates selected and offer feedback on their review sentences.

Module 3: How can I share my thoughts with others?

Activities:

1. Using the review sentences they have written and revised, have students film or voice record their book reviews.
2. Using a QR code generator, link these videos or voice recordings to their own QR code.
3. Tape the QR code to the books or, if not able, have the QR codes printed on cardstock and laminated to hand next to the book with a small picture of the cover attached.
4. Coordinate with a local library, school library, or bookstore to set up a small display in their children's section to display the books with QR codes or the book pictures with QR codes.
5. Set up the displays and write invitations to family, friends, and community members to go and visit the review displays.

Exhibition Event: Students will take their books and reviews and set up their display in the library you have partnered with. Invite friends, family, school peers, and community members to visit the display during its installment to listen to and read the reviews the students created.

Adapting for smaller learning environments: For homeschooling, co-ops, and micro school settings with fewer students, individual students can review multiple books and connect with their local library or bookstore to have their QR codes or written reviews displayed next to their books throughout the library or bookstore.

Pen to Poet

Driving Question: How can we use our imaginations and voices to share our dreams, adventures, and feelings with others?	Public Product: Students will publish a poetry anthology to gift to a loved one.

Unit Overview: Throughout this unit, students will be exposed to a variety of poetry writing styles. They will read mentor texts, analyze poems, and write their own poems. They will compile all their poems into an anthology to give as a gift to a loved one.

Launch Event: Play a short video clip of a poetry performance done by students.

Module 1: What is poetry?

Activities:

1. Gather a variety of poetry books and anthologies to share with students.
2. Spend time reading different poems from different books and anthologies to expose students to a variety of poetry styles.
3. Select a poem with very strong imagery. Provide students with a graphic organizer split into the five senses. As you read the poem aloud, have them record via drawing or writing the different senses they could identify throughout the poem.
4. Select another poem with strong description and imagery and provide a blank piece of paper to students. As you read the poem, have students illustrate the images they see in their mind's eye as the poem is read aloud. Share those illustrations with one another.
5. Read a selection of poems together and take time to discuss the different themes, feelings, messages, and imagery found in the poems.

Module 2: How do you write poems?

Activities:

1. Introduce different styles of poetry and have students use graphic organizers and mentor texts to help craft their own poem of each type.

2. Noun Verb Poem: This is a simple form of poetry that focuses on pairing nouns (names of people, places, or things) with verbs (action words) to create short and descriptive phrases or sentences. The structure of a noun verb poem often consists of short lines of phrases that highlight the relationship between a subject, the noun, and an action, the verb, for example: swings swaying, sun shining, birds chirping, etc.

3. Acrostic Poem: This is a type of poem where certain letters in each line spell out a word or phrase vertically, typically at the beginning of the line. The word or phrase formed by the letters can be the theme of the poem or related to the subject matter such as a person, season, holiday, or place.

4. Color Poem: This is a type of poem that focuses on describing and evoking emotions or sensations associated with a particular color. The poet uses words that make you imagine how that color looks and feels. They use strong and detailed words to bring the color to life in the poem. The goal of a color poem is to show the feeling and meaning of the color using words to help you picture it in your mind, for example, "Red looks like a big fire truck. Red tastes like a crisp apple. Red sounds like a beeping alarm."

5. Rhyming Poem: This is the most common and recognizable type of poem. In rhyming poems words, often at the end of a line, will rhyme with other words within the poem creating a sing song like pattern when read aloud. Rhyming words or phrases can appear throughout a single line, every line, or most commonly, every other line of the poem.

6. Bio Poem: This is short for biographical poem. It is a type of poem that provides a snapshot or overview of a person's life, personality, or character-istics. It is typically written in a simple form that follows specific guidelines for each line of the poem to capture essential information about the subject of the poem.

7. Have students create illustrations to go with their different poems that highlight the topic or feelings behind the poems.

Module 3: How do I share my poems with a loved one?

Activities:

1. After students have written their different poems, show them what a poetry anthology looks like. Explain how an anthology is a collection of works by one author, writing on a similar topic, etc.

2. Have students arrange their poems and illustrations in an order that they would like them published in their own anthology.

(Continued)

3. Have students create a cover that includes an illustration, a title, and their name that will entice a reader to select their anthology to enjoy.
4. Have students create a dedication page to dedicate the work to someone special in their life. This could also be the person they are choosing to gift their anthology to.
5. Create an about the author page, which will be the final page in their book. Have them share a picture of themselves and describe who they are and their interests and accolades similar to other about the author pages in books.
6. Compile all these pages together and staple or bind them together in a creative way.

Exhibition Event: Have students wrap and gift their poetry anthology to a loved one.

No adaptations for alternate learning environments are needed.

Caring for the Earth

Driving Question: How can we inspire others to care for the Earth?	Public Product: Students will create persuasive posters, petitions, books, flyers, etc., to disperse throughout the community to encourage others to participate in actions that support the Earth.

Unit Overview: Throughout this unit, students will identify causes important to them that benefit the Earth. They will learn about different forms of persuasive writing, such as flyers/posters, pamphlets, books, and petitions to help share their initiatives with others. They will pass out their various persuasive writings throughout the community, encouraging others to join them in caring for the Earth.

Launch Event: Write a letter in the voice of Earth asking students to help her with the different problems she is facing, such as lack of clean water, litter, deforestation, pollution.

Module 1: How are humans affecting our planet?

Activities:

1. Begin by having the students generate a list of different problems they see daily that have a negative effect on Earth. Categorize them into problems they see at home, in the classroom, in the community, and in the world.
2. Grab a clipboard, pencil, and piece of paper and survey people asking what problems they see happening that are negatively affecting Earth.
3. Bring the survey results back to the anchor chart and add them to the different categories.

Module 2: What can we do to help our planet?

Activities:

1. Using all the data from Module 1, brainstorm ideas that can help people fix or alter the behaviors that are harming Earth.
2. Select the most important issues from each category or have students pick the ones that are most important to them from each of the categories. Write each at the top of their own piece of paper.

(Continued)

3. Record an idea or two for each of the selected issues that could help people change their behavior or help solve the problem.

Module 3: How can we inspire others to take action, too?

Activities:

1. Discuss the different ways that your voice can be heard when spreading important information and ideas, such as marches, posters, petitions, books/guides, brochures, fliers/pamphlets.

2. Select one of the important issues and have students create posters that they can hang up to spread awareness of the issue and how to take action to make it better. Look at example posters and discuss important features and elements, such as text size, colors, graphics, and messaging.

3. Using another issue they selected, create a petition inviting others to sign and join you in your efforts to make change. Have students take their petitions to recess to spread their ideas and gather signatures from peers that are interested in helping their cause.

4. Pick another issue to write a how-to book/guide. Students should include different steps someone can take to help care for the Earth, such as saving water by turning it off while you brush your teeth, turning the lights off when you leave a room, recycling, picking up litter.

Exhibition Event: Students will deliver their writings and post them in various community spaces such as community centers, city hall, libraries, schools, and popular local businesses to help get the attention of the people in their community and inspire action.

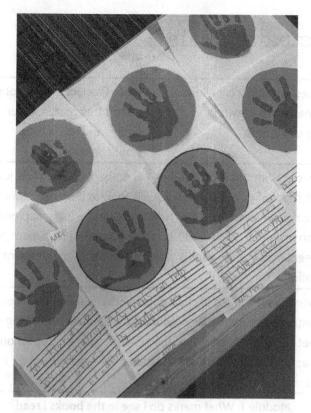

Students create Earth pledges.

Adapting for smaller learning environments: For homeschooling, co-ops, and micro school settings with fewer students, individual students can identify an issue and use that to guide the development of a service project. They can create flyers and informational pamphlets that they can distribute to help spread awareness and invite others to join them.

Punctuation Pals

Driving Question: What are all those different marks in our writing, and how do we use them?	Public Product: A series of classroom posters that feature different punctuation and when they should be used.

Unit Overview: With this unit, students will embark on a learning journey to discover all types of punctuation. They will analyze the use of punctuation in text, discover when to use it and how, and practice using appropriate punctuation in writing. They will then create a series of classroom posters for their peers to use when writing that teaches about the different types of punctuation.

Launch Event: Have a piece of chart paper with multiple sentences all run on together without any punctuation. Students will notice something is off but may not yet know what. Make sure the writing would require various punctuation, such as a period, comma, exclamation mark, question mark, and quotation marks.

Module 1: What marks do I see in the books I read?

Activities:

1. Gather big books or project book pages to make them larger. As you read aloud, ask students if they notice other marks in the writing that are not letters. Use transparent Post-it note arrows to highlight the different punctuation they point out.
2. Print off a short passage with simple sentences and punctuation. Have students read through the passage and highlight the different punctuation they see as they read.
3. Introduce the period. This is a mark that goes at the end of a statement. A statement can be telling someone to do something, an observation, or sharing something you are thinking or doing. This is the most common type of punctuation. Practice generating sentences that would end in a period. Have students go on a period hunt in a book and tally and count how many periods they found in the book.

4. Introduce the exclamation mark. This is a mark that conveys emotion, such as excitement, enthusiasm, danger. It is used at the end of a sentence that requires a louder voice, urgency, or excitement. Practice generating sentences that would end in an exclamation mark. Have students go on an exclamation mark hunt in a book and tally and count how many they found in the book.

5. Introduce the question mark. This is a mark that comes at the end of a question sentence. You use it to ask someone who, what, why, how, where, when, could, should, etc. Practice generating sentences that would end in a question mark. Have students go on a question mark hunt in a book and tally and count how many they found in the book.

6. Introduce commas and quotation marks (optional). These are marks that are very common, but students may or may not fully grasp their use in their own writing, but they will likely recognize them in their reading first. Quotation marks go around the words that someone is speaking. A comma has many different uses, but at this age, you can introduce them as something you use when two sentences are combined using and, or, but, or also when someone is listing things. Practice generating sentences that would use commas or quotation marks. Have students go on a mark hunt in a book and tally and count how many they found in the book.

Module 2: How do I use these marks in my writing?

Activities:

1. Print out a variety of sentences on strips of paper, and then write different punctuation on small squares of paper or Post-it notes. Have students place the appropriate punctuation at the end of each sentence and explain why they chose it.

2. Read aloud sentences from favorite story books with a variety of punctuation endings and have students write the punctuation mark they would use on a white board and then reveal the correct mark and check if they were correct.

3. Have students work on a variety of writing, such as letters, cards, notes, and stories, finding and using the correct punctuation throughout.

4. Have students review and revise their previous writing to find where punctuation is missing or where incorrect punctuation was used.

(Continued)

Module 3: How can I help others remember when and how to use punctuation?
Activities: 1. Divide students into groups and assign them a specific punctuation mark. 2. Have students begin with a rough draft for their punctuation poster where they will write the name of the mark, draw a picture of the mark, write when to use it, and write a sample sentence using it appropriately. 3. Have students hunt in books for examples of their punctuation mark used correctly. Scan or photograph the sentences. 4. On their final poster, have them transfer the information from their rough draft and use markers to make their writing and pictures stand out. Have them cut out the example sentences form books to glue to the poster as well.
Exhibition Event: Students will present their posters to their peers and hang them in the classroom to reference during writing time.

Adapting for smaller learning environments: For homeschooling, co-ops, and micro school settings with fewer students, individual students will make a poster for each mark and/or create a punctuation reference sheet that they can keep in their writing folder/journal.

Did They Learn Their Lesson?

Driving Question: How can we bring our favorite stories to life?	Public Product: Students will perform a reader's theater based on favorite fairy tales and fables.

Unit Overview: Throughout this unit, students will learn about the magic of storytelling through fables and fairy tales. They will investigate theme, characters, morals, and lessons learned thorough the events of the story. They will create props and costumes, build their oral speaking skills, and perform a reader's theater piece for friends and family.

Launch Event: Watch a short video clip of a child-friendly theater production showing how people act and perform on stage.

Module 1: What makes a story fun to tell and share with others?

Activities:

1. Reread the story that has been selected for the reader's theater. Story map the book by recording characters (main, secondary, protagonist, antagonist), settings, and a simple plot outline of the beginning, middle, and end.
2. Explore the characters in the book. Who are they? What role do they play? Create character trait webs for the main characters.
3. Discuss the story's moral/theme. What lesson do the characters learn? Why is telling this story important?
4. Rewrite the story in a story board fashion. What main events will you include in your reader's theater? What scenes do you want to include? What settings will be in your performance? What main events will you include?

Module 2: How can we use our voices and bodies to share a story with others?

Activities:

1. Prewrite short scripts for students for each scene they put on their story-board. Differentiate for different reading readiness.
2. Practice reading lines chorally, repeat after me, in partners, etc.
3. Practice vocal expression. How does the character sound: loud, quiet, slow, fast? Happy, sad, excited, scared, surprised?
4. Act out the movements of different characters and scenes.

(Continued)

5. Practice the script all the way through, giving gentle feedback and tips to encourage confidence. Remind students to be loud, use movements, and show emotion.

Module 3: How can we create a reader's theater experience?
Activities: 1. Using donated clothing and fabric, have students design their costumes. 2. Create props with recyclable materials. 3. Design and create different backdrops and scenery pieces for the various settings and scenes. 4. Rehearse with props, costumes, and scene changes. 5. Create invitations for others to attend your reader's theater.
Exhibition Event: Students will invite family and friends to their reader's theater performance.

Using manipulatives, students reenact fables and fairytales.

Adapting for smaller learning environments: For homeschooling, co-ops, and micro school settings with fewer students, individual students can create a puppet show or various characters out of paper attached to popsicle sticks.

Nature Lovers Hiking Guide

Driving Question: How can we help families find fun, safe places to explore nature?	Public Product: Students will produce a kid-friendly hiking guide that they will make available to local and visiting families.

Unit Overview: During this unit, students will become nature explorers and will embark on a series of different local hikes. They will learn about hiking safety, trail features, and local wildlife and nature. Students will rate the hikes on a scale of easiest to hardest for kids, note their different features, and photograph the hikes. They will compile it in a hiking guidebook for families to help them select hikes they can do with their children.

Launch Event: Begin by doing a simple walk around the school campus and neighborhood. Stop periodically to ask, "What do you see? What do you hear? What makes this a fun place to explore?" to get students noticing what makes exploring and walking fun for them.

Module 1: What makes a hike fun and safe for kids?

Activities:

1. Discuss different safety basics and make a poster together of the things students need to remember when they go on a hiking trail. (Staying on the designated trail, wearing the right shoes, bringing water, hiking with an adult.)
2. Create a hiking safety checklist with quick symbols to go with each one.
3. Take students on local kid-friendly trail hikes. On each hike, have students document the trail, different features, the parking, trailhead, spots to rest, views, etc., by taking photographs.
4. Have students take notes about trail features such as signs, interesting nature, landmarks, such as bridges, large rocks, and ponds, to use in their hiking guide.
5. After each hike, create an anchor chart for the trail that answers questions like "What did you like about the trail? Was it easy to walk? What interesting or cool things did you see on the hike? Were you out of breath during the hike?" and record this information on the chart for future guide pages.
6. Print off some of the photos to attach to the trail's anchor chart.
7. Using a map of the trail printed out, work together to mark where different interesting and notable features were at along the trail.

(Continued)

Module 2: How can we show other kids what makes a trail exciting to explore?
Activities:
1. Have students choose their favorite feature of the hike and draw a detailed illustration of the feature.
2. Use sentence frames such as "My favorite part was. . ..," "I saw. . ..," or "This hike had. . .." to help students describe their experiences on the hike to include in the hiking guide.
3. Have students create captions for the photographs taken on the different hikes.
4. Create a rating scale from one to five, one being the easiest and five being the hardest, and establish criteria for each rating.
5. Rate each hike using the rating scale created.
Module 3: How can we share our hiking adventures with others?
Activities:
1. Create a hiking guide page template that includes the name of the hike, location/address, rating, description, photographs, drawings of landmarks, and student quotes. This can take more than one page.
2. Using the information compiled on the anchor charts for each hike, assign small groups to each hike to create the hiking page for that trail.
3. Compile all the hiking guide pages together and make multiple copies.
4. Have students create covers for the hiking guides and bind or staple them altogether.
Exhibition Event: Coordinate with local outdoor businesses, City Hall, tourism department, national parks, etc., to disperse your hiking guides for the public to have access to. Consider also making it available online to reach a wider audience.

While out on a hike, students record their observations to include in their hiking guides.

Adapting for smaller learning environments: For homeschooling, co-ops, and micro school settings with fewer students, individual students can create a page for each hike you go on. This could also be a year-long ongoing project that you are working on alongside other units that are isolated throughout the year.

Silent Stories

Driving Question: How can we tell a story without using words?	Public Product: Students will publish a wordless picture book.

Unit Overview: Throughout this unit, students will explore the power of storytelling through pictures. They will learn about how illustrations can convey emotions, actions, and events to tell a story without any words. Students will study wordless picture books, learn the art of illustration, and plan and organize their own stories. It will all culminate in the publishing of their own wordless picture book that they will present during a storytelling showcase and then partner with their local library to put their books into circulation.

Launch Event: Watch a short video clip of a wordless cartoon.

Module 1: How do pictures show what happens in a story?

Activities:

1. Start by talking with students about the cartoon they watched. What was the plot of the storyline? How could they tell what was happening even without any words? Could they tell how the characters were feeling? How so?

2. Read together through different wordless picture books. Stop at various places to talk about what is happening in the story and what evidence in the illustration tells them that information. Discuss how the pictures change from one page to the next but how the details about the pictures stay the same, such as the characters, the appearance of the characters and setting, the colors and feel of the illustrations.

3. Print out sequencing pictures of someone doing something, such as getting ready for bed, building a sandcastle at the beach, getting their snow clothes on. Provide the picture cards to the students and have them sequence them in order. Then ask them to describe why they put the cards in that order. What from the pictures gave them clues about what order they should go in?

4. Do an emotions sort where you provide pictures of people feeling different emotions in different ways. Have them sort into categories: happy, sad, angry, etc. Have students talk about the features of the face and body language that led them to sort the picture the way they did.

5. Provide three pieces of paper to all students. Have them try out drawing their first mini picture story of something simple like a ball being thrown or jumping into the water. Then have them present these short stories to a partner to talk about how their story starts, what happens in the middle, and how they end.

6. Read students a story without showing them the pictures. Have them then take time to draw the illustrations for the story to retell in only images.

Module 2: How can we use pictures to create our own story?

Activities:

1. Using a story map graphic organizer, have students plan their characters, setting, problem, and solution.

2. Have students touch and plan across multiple pages of their story. Using Post-it notes, they can do rough sketches for what will happen across multiple pages.

3. Have students start by drawing their characters across each page. What actions are they doing? What expressions should they have? How are they interacting with one another?

4. Have students add in their settings. Where are they? What season? What time of day? What's the weather? All of this can be show by adding specific details throughout the pictures.

5. Have students use strategic marks to show movement of their characters.

6. Have students meet with a partner to go through their books. Have the partner tell what he or she thinks is happening on each page. If they have questions or confusion, have the students use that as an opportunity for revision and to add more detail to make their story clearer.

Module 3: How can we share our books with others?

Activities:

1. Before adding color to the illustrations, take a picture walk through the mentor texts again to notice the quality of the coloring and the consistency of color throughout. For example, the main character's shirt is always red, their hair is always black, etc.

2. Take multiple days to thoughtfully and carefully add color to their illustrations. This can be with crayon, marker, colored pencil, or watercolors.

3. Use a black fine point felt tip pen to outline the illustration details to make them stand out more. (If using crayon to color, you will want to do the outline prior to coloring.)

(Continued)

4. Study covers of different books. Discuss the elements that make a book cover, such as a title, name of author and illustrator, an illustration that goes with the story but doesn't give it away. Design and color covers for their books.
5. Using a spiral binder, add a plastic sheet to the beginning and end of the book and carefully bind the stories.

Exhibition Event: Take an expedition to the local library to submit your books for circulation or to set up a temporary display of the books for others to enjoy when they are at the library.

No adaptations needed for alternative learning environments.

06 Cross-Curricular PBL Units

Learning is most meaningful when subjects connect, allowing children to see how different skills and ideas work together in the real world. Young learners naturally make these connections, counting while they build, telling stories about their drawings, or exploring science through hands-on play. Project-Based Learning (PBL) embraces this holistic approach by blending subjects into engaging, hands-on experiences that make learning more cohesive, relevant, and fun. Instead of separating math, science, literacy, and social studies into isolated lessons, children engage in real-world projects that bring multiple subjects together in a natural and meaningful way.

The following units are designed to help preschool and kindergarten learners build foundational skills across multiple subject areas. Through hands-on, inquiry-driven projects, students will see how subjects overlap, strengthen their problem-solving skills, and develop a deeper understanding of the world around them.

Jr. Photographer

Driving Question: How can we use photography to show the beauty of nature in our community?	Public Product: Students will create a nature photography calendar to sell to their family, friends, and other community members to raise money for expeditions and project supplies for the school year.

Unit Overview: Throughout this unit, students will become nature photographers and explore the beauty of the natural world in their own back yard. Through nature walks, observation, and photography, students will capture photographs of plants, trees, animals, weather, and other nature elements to be compiled into a calendar with each month featuring different student photographs and captions.

Launch Event: Show extreme close-up photographs of nature elements and have students guess what they think it is a picture of. Then zoom out or show a regular photo of it to check if they were correct.

Module 1: What makes nature beautiful and interesting to photograph?

Activities:

1. Provide students with small nature journals, or paper stapled together, to take on a nature walk. As you walk, ask students to draw what they see: birds, leaves, flowers, trees, insects, rocks, etc. Encourage them to notice the tiny details, such as color, texture, pattern.
2. Set up a "look closely" station where students can observe natural objects: leaves, pinecones, rocks, bark, seeds, etc. Include magnifying glasses to explore items closely and notice their details.
3. Take students outside with color charts or paint sample strips from a hardware store. Challenge them to find things in nature that match each color.
4. Provide an assortment of nature magazines or magazines with nature photographs in them. Have students cut out and create a nature photography inspiration poster. Ask students to share about why they selected the photograph, meaning what made it beautiful to them?
5. Read books and show photographs of nature in different seasons. Talk about how nature elements change. Have students notice what season it is currently and talk about how what they see might change over time.

Module 2: How can we take quality photos of nature to show its beauty?

Activities:

1. Introduce how to safely hold a camera or tablet. Explain how to point it toward what they want to take a picture of, hold it steady, and press the button to take the photograph.
2. Teach students how to "frame" their picture. Cut out "frames" from old cereal boxes and have them practice framing different objects around the classroom. Remind them that if they don't see it inside of the frame it will not be in the picture.
3. Set up a small indoor "nature photo studio" with items like flowers, shells, and leaves. Students practice taking close-up photos of objects. Discuss which photos they like best and why.
4. Take students on a photo walk around the playground or a local park. Give student each the time to take two or three photographs. When you return to the classroom, go through the photos together and talk about what they like about the photos.
5. Head out on another nature walk or short hike, this time allowing students time to take up to five photos each of things they find beautiful in nature.

Module 3: How do we create a calendar that is helpful to others?

Activities:

1. Have students select their best photo or two to submit to the calendar. Print out selected photos.
2. Have students write a one-sentence caption to go with their photograph/s that tell what they took a picture of and why.
3. Have students use their printed photographs and captions to design each month's photo collage and the cover.
4. Digitally recreate the student's design in a calendar making software.
5. Print and bind multiple copies of the calendar.
6. Have students go through the calendars and mark important or fun national days or holidays in the calendar with small stickers.
7. Create posters to advertise their calendars and ask for donations for purchasing the calendars. Use the funds for future expedition costs and needed supplies.

Exhibition Event: Students will partner with a local print shop or business to print and bind their calendars. Then hang their posters to collect donations for their calendars and distribute them to family, friends, and community members to raise money for their future expeditions and needed PBL supplies for the year.

While on expeditions, students take turn photographing nature elements.

Adapting for smaller learning environments: For homeschooling, co-ops, and micro school settings with fewer students, individual students can select their best photograph for each month and distribute their calendars to family and friends.

My Five Senses

Driving Question: How can we help others experience their five senses?	Public Product: Students will design, create and facilitate an interactive sensory walk.

Unit Overview: Throughout this unit, students will explore their five senses. They will identify their senses and understand what activates each of those senses. They will use their experiences and research to create an interactive sensory experience for others to use to learn about their five senses.

Launch Event: As students enter the learning space, have lights dimmed and dinosaur sounds playing in the background.

Module 1: What are our senses?

Activities:

1. Introduce the different senses: taste, touch, see, hear, smell.
2. Create an anchor chart divided into five parts or a small chart for each sense. Have students brainstorm different objects for each sense, for example, flower for sell, rainbow for see, cat for touch, guitar for hear, lemon for taste.
3. Read nonfiction books about the five senses and add new objects to the anchor chart.
4. Provide a senses sort for students to sort objects into different sense groups.
5. Have students draw or provide a template for a human body. Have them label the different senses on the body and create a five senses diagram.

Module 2: How do our senses help us?

Activities:

1. Sight exploration day: Go on a color walk and have students find objects for each color of the rainbow. Gather objects and compare their visible similarities and differences. Put out puzzles and other visual discrimination activities and games for students to explore.
2. Hearing exploration day: Play short clips of different sounds, such as sirens, birds, cars, clapping, rain and have students listen and guess the sound. Make instruments out of recycled materials, such as guitars, rain sticks, and drums. Using small opaque containers, fill pairs with the same materials and have students shake and match by sound. Compare loud vs. quiet sounds.

(Continued)

3. Taste exploration day: Create a diagram of the tongue for each type of taste and sample foods that fit in each category. Set up blind tasting where students will taste different things and pair them with their taste match. Do a taste test survey where students will ask people what their favorite taste is out of four options. Graph the data.
4. Smell exploration day: Place spices, foods, oils, etc., of different scents in opaque bottles. Have students smell them and find their match or match them to a picture of the scent. Make scented Play-Doh and have students enjoy a scent filled sensory time. Print pictures of different scents and have students sort them into pleasant or unpleasant scent.
5. Touch exploration day: Create a mystery box with objects with different textures. Have students reach in to feel and guess the object or put two of each object in and have the feel and find the match. Provide items that have a variety of textures for students to explore, such as soft, rough, smooth, bumpy, pokey. Make texture rubbings of objects with crayons; use leaves, bark, tiles, sandpaper, stencils, etc.

Module 3: How can we share the senses with others?

Activities:

1. Divide students into small groups and assign them each one of the five senses.
2. Have students brainstorm an interactive activity they could create for others to experience their sense as in these five examples. Sight: a light table with colorful objects, mirrors, and manipulatives. Hearing: shakers and recorded nature sounds. Smell: smelling jars with pictures to match to the scent. Touch: a feeling wall with different textures for people to experience. Taste: safe and simple foods to sample such as lemon juice, salted chip, etc.
3. Have students create the materials needed for their sensory station.
4. Create visual instructions using drawings or photographs that show others how to explore their station.
5. Make a welcome sign and posters to invite others to experience their sensory walk.

Exhibition Event: Students will invite school community, family, and friends to come and experience the sensory walk. Have students act as tour guides to take their guests through each station.

Adapting for smaller learning environments: For homeschooling, co-ops, and micro school settings with fewer students, individual students can create a small station for each of the senses and give tours to siblings, friends, neighbors, and family.

Meet Me at the Museum

Driving Question: How did dinosaurs use their unique characteristics and adaptations?	Public Product: Students will produce a dinosaur museum presentation with 3-D models, habitat dioramas, and museum placards or videos with facts and information presented by the students.

Unit Overview: Throughout this unit, students will explore dinosaurs and what made each one unique. They will learn about dinosaur characteristics and adaptations, investigate where different dinosaurs lived, and discover how we know so much about these prehistoric creatures today. They will use their research and creativity to design a museum exhibit complete with 3D dinosaur models, habitat dioramas, and informational placards or videos to help others learn all about dinosaurs.

Launch Event: To spark excitement and curiosity, transform your classroom into a pop-up fossil site! As students arrive, greet them with excavation hats or badges and invite them to a large sand or sensory bin filled with hidden "fossils" (plastic bones, shells, small dinosaur toys, etc.). After a short dig, gather the group and pose a mystery: *"What kind of creatures left these behind? And how do we know anything about them if they're no longer here?"*

Module 1: What makes a dinosaur unique?

Activities:

1. Begin with a Know, Wonder, Learn (KWL) schema map where students will begin by sharing all they already know about dinosaurs to record in the K (know) column. Then, generate questions that they have about dinosaurs and write them in the W (wonder) column. Throughout the unit record new learning and facts in the L (learn) column.
2. Using nonfiction books and video clips, research a variety of dinosaurs students are interested in.
3. Compare and contrast various dinosaurs and what features they have in common, and what features are unique to specific dinosaurs.
4. Print pictures of dinosaurs to glue to a large chart and label their unique features as a diagram.
5. Using air dry clay, create 3-D models of favorite dinosaurs, paint them realistically based on their research, and make sure to include their specific attributes.

(Continued)

Module 2: Where did dinosaurs live?
Activities:
1. Research through shared reading of nonfiction books, websites, and video clips about dinosaur habitats.
2. Talk about the various vegetation, water sources, terrain, etc., that dinosaurs may have lived in and around.
3. Revisit the different attributes dinosaurs have and make connections to their habitat. What adaptations did dinosaurs have that helped them survive in their habitat?
4. Gather items from nature and recyclable items and create 3-D replicas of dinosaur habitats for student's 3-D dinosaur models.
Module 3: How do we know so much about dinosaurs?
Activities:
1. Organize a virtual call with a paleontologist or find a video clip about the job of a paleontologist. Learn about their role in discovering, recovering, and preserving dinosaur remains.
2. Set up excavation stations for students to practice their skills excavating "remains."
3. Draw, dictate, or write a museum plaque for the dinosaur and habitat they selected. Include a drawing, a few sentences, a map of where remains can be found, and their footprint.
4. Set up displays of their museum plaque, 3-D dinosaur sculpture, and habitat diorama.
Exhibition Event: Students will give museum tours to school community, friends, and family, teaching others about dinosaur's unique features and adaptations, their habitats, and how they were discovered.

Students observe dinosaur bones.

Adapting for smaller learning environments: For homeschooling, co-ops, and micro school settings with fewer students, individual students can create multiple displays or create a video presentation of their display to send to friends and family members.

Let's Grow Food

Driving Question: How can we work together to grow plants that help our community?	Public Product: Students will design, plant, and grow a community garden.

Unit Overview: In this unit, students will learn about plants, how they grow, and how gardens can help a community. As a team, they will design and build a community garden and take on the role of a gardener, growing plants that can help people, animals, and insects in their community.

Launch Event: Have a variety of fresh fruits and vegetables that can be grown in a garden where you live. Have students taste them and identify what they are.

Module 1: What do plants need to live and grow?

Activities:

1. Introduce the parts of a plant (roots, stem, leaves, flowers, fruit, etc.). Using pictures of plants, have students label and create a diagram.
2. Conduct an experiment to learn about what plants need to survive. In one cup plant a seed (lima beans and radishes grow quickly) and give it sunlight, water, and soil. In another cup, place the seed without necessary resources. Watch as one grows and one does not.
3. Read books about how plants grow and the life cycle of plants.
4. Have students create plant starts and observe and record the changes they see in their plant over time.
5. Using the plant starts, begin to brainstorm a list of foods that could be grown in a garden where you live.

Module 2: How can we plan and prepare a garden?

Activities:

1. Print out or show a variety of map styles. Discuss which type of map would be best for designing and planning your garden (bird's eye view).
2. Identify where your garden will be placed, then draw the shape of your garden onto a large piece of chart paper.
3. Begin to draw sections of the garden and identify what plants will grow in each section. Have students label the map with words and drawings of the plant for each section.

4. Draw, or print out to color, pictures of each plant that will be growing in your garden. Have students color and label, laminate, and attach to a craft stick to create garden labels for the soil.
5. Introduce and discuss the different tools and materials you will need to plant and care for a garden. How are they used and why are they important?
6. Gather soil, fertilizer, seeds, gloves, shovels, watering cans, and other tools and supplies needed for garden planting day.
7. Work as a class to create a "garden rules" poster that can be hung in the garden space, so others know how to work in or enjoy the garden without harming the growing plants.
8. Create a garden jobs poster that assigns different students different roles in caring for the garden.

Module 3: How can we care for our garden and share it with others?

Activities:

1. Planting Day! Have students plant flowers, herbs, vegetables, fruits, etc. according to the map they designed in Module 2. Label with the garden label stakes they created in Module 2.
2. Create a garden care schedule that rotates the garden jobs from Module 2 to give every student an opportunity to care for the garden in some capacity, such as watering, pulling weeds, harvesting.
3. Visit the garden daily to observe changes. Make plans for when you notice plants that are struggling and may need more support.
4. Create decorations for the garden such as painted rocks, signs, pinwheels, garlands, etc., for the grand opening of their garden.
5. Create and distribute flyers and invitations for the garden grand opening party.

Exhibition Event: Invite school community, family, friends, and community members to the grand opening of the community garden. Have students give tours of the variety of plants they planted, talk about their garden design, share about how they have cared for the garden, and have samples of the different foods planted in the garden.

Students created garden stakes to mark the types of food they are growing and where they planted them.

Adapting for smaller learning environments: For homeschooling, co-ops, and micro school settings with fewer students, individual students can design and plant a small garden at their home or in a local community garden plot. Share the harvest with loved ones and neighbors.

Light and Shadows

Driving Question: How do light and shadows create art?	Public Product: Students will guide others through a light and shadow interactive art gallery.
Unit Overview: With this unit, students will explore the relationship of light and shadows. Through observation, experiments, and creative play, students will discover how light behaves, how shadows are made, and how light and dark can work together to create beautiful art. Students will work together to create art installations that use light and shadow in creative ways, and will culminate in an interactive gallery that they will guide others through to experience the relationship between light and shadows.	
Launch Event: Read aloud the book *Moonbear's Shadow* by Frank Asch or *The Black Rabbit* by Philippa Leathers. Talk about the shadows, where they think they came from and what they are.	

Module 1: What are shadows and how are they made?

Activities:

1. Set up a light and shadow sensory station where students can explore light in a hands-on, creative play way. Include small flashlights, lamps, light table/tablet, translucent and opaque manipulatives, etc.
2. Conduct an experiment using a flashlight and a small object to explore how moving the object closer to or farther from the light source will impact the size of the shadow. Have students make predictions about what will happen as they move the objects closer and farther away from the flashlight.
3. Place toys or objects on a large piece of paper for each student. Project light toward the objects and toys and have students trace the shadows as they appear on the page.
4. Using crayon, marker, or paint sticks, have students color in the shadow drawings and trace them with black marker.
5. Go outside on a sunny day to observe and play with shadows. Have students trace each other's shadows in cool poses on the cement.
6. Have students cut shapes from old cereal boxes or card stock paper and use flashlights to cast shadows on the wall and create a shadow puppet.

(Continued)

181

Module 2: How does light help us see colors, shapes, and patterns?

Activities:

1. Provide students with materials like clear plastic, tissue paper, fabric, and cardboard. Shine light through the different materials and observe what happens. What can light shine through? What blocks the light? Introduce vocabulary like opaque, translucent, and transparent.

2. Create stained glass art to include in the installation. Look at pictures of stained glass windows to talk about the colors and how the light impacts the color. Use tissue paper or colored cellophane to create patterns on clear contact paper. Hang the art in windows to observe how the light travels through the different colors.

3. Explore how light bounces and reflects by shining light on hand mirrors. Ask students about what they observe happening when light shines on a mirror and how they think they can make the light move and bounce to a new place.

4. Investigate the effect of color on light by placing colored cellophane in front of white light. Compare and contrast the shadows created by the colored light vs. non colored light.

5. Using a prism, CD disc, or water filled glass, use light from the sun or a flashlight to explore making rainbows. Have students create rainbow inspired art to add to the gallery.

Module 3: How can we create art using light and shadows?

Activities:

1. Have students use a variety of objects and create a scene along the edge of their paper. Have a partner hold a flashlight so they can trace their shadow scene onto a piece of paper. Have students also snap a photograph of their shadow scene. Then have them color in their outlines with black marker.

2. Create layered shadows by cutting out a design from black paper and gluing them on to white paper. Then glue a piece of white tissue paper or vellum on top of the design. Cut another design out of black paper to glue on top of the vellum. Glue another piece of vellum as another layer on top. Finally, cut one more design out of black paper to glue on the top layer. This will mimic the different depths of shadow and light.

3. Have students cut shapes out of a piece of card stock paper. Then have them cut and glue colored cellphone over each hole they cut out. Take the mats outside and hold under the sun to project a colored design on the concrete. Have students take photographs of each other's shadow art to include in the installation.
4. Gather artwork from this and all previous modules.
5. Design and create an interactive experience for guests of the gallery. This could be a table with student made shadow puppets and a flashlight, a light table with a. variety of manipulative objects, of a mirror and light station with flashlights, mirrors, prisms, CD discs, etc. for participants to explore bouncing and refracting light.
6. Have students design and assemble the gallery, and practice presenting the different art installations.

Exhibition Event: Invite school community, friends, family, and community members to explore the light and shadow art gallery and interactive exhibit. Have students act as tour guides to usher guests through the different stations and exhibits.

Adapting for smaller learning environments: For homeschooling, co-ops, and micro school settings with fewer students, individual students can invite siblings, cousins, friends, and neighbors to experience their light and shadow exhibit.

Explore the Rainbow

Driving Question: How can we find, explore, and use color to make something beautiful and useful for our classroom?	Public Product: Students will create color posters for their classroom for students to reference throughout the school year.

Unit Overview: In this unit, students will learn about colors through observation, hands-on activities, and art making. They will find colors in their everyday environment, experiment with color mixing, and use color to create art. The unit will culminate with students creating color collage posters that will hang in their classroom to help one another recognize and identify colors and write the color words.

Launch Event:

Module 1: Where do we see colors around us?

Activities:

1. Set up baskets labeled with different colors. Then provide a basket full of objects that match those different colors. Have students sort the objects into the correct color category.

2. Using an old egg carton, have students use markers to color the bottom of each section a different color. Then, outside or in the classroom, go on a color hunt and find one small object to put in each section to match the colors. Return to the gathering space to share some of the items found for each color.

3. Read aloud popular children's books that focus on color such as these: *Brown Bear, Brown Bear, What Do You See?* by Eric Carle, *Mouse Paint* by Ellen Stoll Walks, *Colors Everywhere* by Tana Hoban, etc.

4. Make sensory color bottles by filling clear bottles with water, food coloring, and glitter or beads all the same color per bottle. Super glue the lids on and let students observe and experiment with the bottles and discuss the colors they see.

5. Set up a color exploration station with a variety of blocks, manipulatives, and other stem materials that are all different colors.

Module 2: How can we mix and make new colors?

Activities:

1. Provide red, yellow, and blue paint. Learn about how these three are the primary colors and they are the three colors that make all other colors they see. Allow students to experiment with mixing two colors together to see what other new colors they can make. Once they make purple, green, and orange, learn about how they are secondary colors, the colors made by mixing two primary colors together.

2. Give each student a coffee filter, washable markers, and water eye droppers with a small dish of clean water. Have students color the filters with different colors, trying not to overlap the colors. Then have students use the water droppers to carefully drop water on the coffee filter. Discuss the observations of what students see happening to the coffee filter and the colors as the water is dropped on.

3. Using clear cups with clean water, food coloring, and eye droppers, have students observe what happens when food coloring is added to the clear water. Then have them use eye droppers to mix two different colors of water together in a fresh cup. What colors can they create?

4. Provide stations for students to have hands-on exploration with mixing colors to create new. This could include a finger-painting station, a play dough mixing station, or a watercolor painting station.

Module 3: How can we help others learn about the colors we have made?

Activities:

1. Gather a variety of magazines, old books, images, and colored paper.
2. Assign groups of students to a specific color and give them a large piece of paper to create their classroom color posters.
3. Draw the name of the color on the top of the poster to have students color in and design with crayons or markers in the shade of that color.
4. Have students go through the materials provided and cut or tear out anything that is the color of their team's poster.
5. Collage and glue these clippings to completely fill the paper with their color.

Exhibition Event: Students will present their posters to their peers and hang them in the classroom for students to reference.

Students sort objects by color.

Students discern different shades of colors.

Adapting for smaller learning environments: For homeschooling, co-ops, and micro school settings with fewer students, individual students can create a color poster that has a small collage area for each color and label or smaller posters for each color to hang in their learning space.

Trip to the Toy Store

Driving Question: How can we design, create, and share toys that other kids will enjoy?	Public Product: Students will create their very own toy, advertise it to others, and put them in a classroom toy store for dramatic play use.

Unit Overview: In this unit, students will become young inventors, designers, and marketers as they explore what makes a toy fun, engaging, and meaningful. Students will brainstorm toy ideas, learn about toy design, and use materials to create their own toys. They will also explore the concept of marketing, creating signs, posters, and even simple commercials to share their toys with others. Finally, the classroom will transform into a dramatic play toy store, where students will set up displays and practice selling their creations to their peers.

Launch Event: Set up stations with various types of popular or unique toys, such as a building station with blocks and other building toys, doll station with dolls, Barbie's, and other doll-like toys, puzzle and game station, and artistic toys: Play-Doh, easels, Spirograph, animal play with figurines and animal related toys, and more. Have students rotate through the stations to experience the different types of toys.

Module 1: What makes a toy fun, and can we create our own?

Activities:

1. After exploring all the toy stations, have students gather to discuss and create a chart about what makes a toy fun to play with. What did they like about specific toys at each station? What made them play with them, and play with them for a long time? What makes them want to go back and play with a toy again?

2. Brainstorm as a class what types of toys they might want to create. What category would their toy fit into? Would it be a toy for one player or would multiple people play with it together? What kinds of materials could it be made from?

3. Take time for students to create detailed and labeled sketches of their toy design. Have them label different features of the toy like on/off switch, volume, real working light, four game pieces, etc.

(Continued)

4. Have students present their toy design ideas to small groups or the whole group. Have students ask one another questions about their toy or offer kind suggestions about how to make it even better.
5. Return to their sketches to make alterations to their designs based on the feedback and questions.
6. Provide a variety of craft materials and recyclable materials for students to use to create their toy.
7. Have a toy testing day where students can pair up and test each other's toys and give each other feedback. Make needed alterations to the toys.

Module 2: How do we show others our toy is special?

Activities:

1. Show students toy packaging, posters, advertisements, and simple commercials. Have a discussion about how these elements made them feel: did they make them want the toy, did it make them excited to play with the toy?
2. Talk about the elements on the packaging, advertisements, and in the commercials that are used specifically for marketing the toy: colors, font size, designs, how the people speak, volume, etc.
3. Have students design and create a poster for their toy. Have them include a picture of their toy and simple phrases to draw in attention. Include color and design that catches the eye and entices people to way to have their toy.
4. Create short video clip commercials where students show and name their toy, show how to play with it, and tell others why they should want it.
5. Create an advertisement for their toy on a small index card. Then, glue the index cards to plain printer paper to create a toy catalogue of all the toys made in the class.
6. Create price tags and sale signs for their toy.

Module 3: What makes a good toy store?
Activities:

1. Take an expedition to a local toy store or a toy section of a store. Have students take note of how toys are organized and displayed, the signage, and details of the way the toys are shown.
2. Back at school, design what they want their toy store space to look like. Work together to create a map of where shelves and tables will go, what types of toys will go where, where the check-out station will be, etc.
3. Have students design and create decorations for their toy store, including posters, signs, price tags, sale signs, etc.
4. Have students work together to set up and decorate their toy shop dramatic play center. Have them display their toys, hang posters, put out their catalogues and price tags, and make their store fun and inviting.
5. Create play money that students can use to "buy" the toys during their play center time.
6. Create job tags that students will wear when they play in the toy shop space, so all know their role, such as shopper, cashier, stocker.
7. Co-create a toy store play rules poster that outlines the expectations for play in that area. Have all students sign the agreement so they understand how they should respect and treat the space and the materials in it.

Exhibition Event: Open the toy shop play space for use during open-ended play time in class. Allow students to sign up for the days they want to play and help facilitate play in the toy shop.

Adapting for smaller learning environments: For homeschooling, co-ops, and micro school settings with fewer students, individual students can create multiple toys and/or make a toy and include toys they already own to set up a toy store play space. Invite friends for a play date to play in your pretend store!

07 Crafting Your Own PBL Unit

Project-Based Learning (PBL) makes learning come alive. It turns everyday moments into meaningful experiences, where kids aren't just memorizing, they're exploring, creating, and making connections that stick. Whether they're measuring ingredients for a class cookbook, building bridges to test weight, or mapping their neighborhood, PBL gives them a reason to be excited about learning. It shows them that their learning has real world applications, and what they learn matters outside the walls of their classroom.

Now that you've got a variety of ready-to-go units to choose from, why not jump in and try one? Pick a topic that sparks interest, see how your students respond, and journey together through each of the unit's modules and lessons. Once you have a unit or two under your belt, you're ready to try your hand at creating your own and I am going to teach you how to design your own PBL units from scratch! With a little planning and creativity, you can create projects that fit your students, your classroom, and your teaching style. Let's get started!

Let's be real, planning a full PBL unit can feel overwhelming if you're not sure where to start. But here's the secret: **start with the end in mind!** Backward planning is a framework that takes the guesswork out of designing a PBL unit by focusing on your ultimate learning goals from the very beginning. It ensures that your activities and lessons aren't just random, disconnected experiences but are instead purposeful steps that lead your students toward deeper learning and a meaningful final product.

If you've ever felt like your project ideas fizzle out or don't have a clear direction, **backward planning is your solution!**

What Is Backward Planning

Backward planning (also known as backward design) is a method where you begin by identifying the **learning goals** you want your students to achieve by the end of the project and then work backward to plan the activities, experiences, and assessments that will get them there.

Table 7-1 shows how backward planning differs from chronological or traditional planning.

Example: Let's say you're planning a project around **Community Helpers.**

- **Traditional Planning:** You pick a theme, like "Community Helpers," and plan activities around it (reading a book about firefighters, making a police officer craft, etc.). Each activity stands alone, and there's no clear connection between them.
- **Backward Planning:** You start by identifying the learning goal: "Students will understand the roles of community helpers and why they're important." Then you plan a project where students explore community helpers through meaningful experiences, like interviewing a local firefighter, creating a community map, or designing a care package for healthcare workers.

Backward planning is the secret to creating intentional, meaningful PBL units that engage young learners and meet their developmental needs. When you start with the end in mind, you'll find that your unit flows naturally, and your students will be more engaged, motivated, and excited to learn.

Table 7-1   Traditional vs. Backward Planning

Traditional (Chronological) Planning	Backward Planning (Backward Design)
Starts with planning activities and lessons.	Starts with identifying learning goals.
Focuses on covering content step-by-step.	Focuses on achieving specific outcomes.
May result in disconnected activities.	Ensures activities are purposeful and aligned.
Assessment happens at the end.	Assessment is planned from the beginning.
Teacher-directed.	Student-centered and inquiry based.

The following sections explain what backward planning looks like In a PBL unit.

Start with the End in Mind

Think about what you want your students to know, understand, and be able to do by the time the project is finished.

- Are you focusing on literacy, math, or science standards?
- Are there specific social-emotional skills you want to build?
- Do you want your students to work on problem-solving, critical thinking, or collaboration?

Once you know your goals, you can ensure that every part of your project supports those outcomes.

Determine How You'll Measure Success

What does success look like in your PBL unit? How will students demonstrate their learning? In early childhood classrooms, authentic assessments are much more meaningful than traditional tests. Think about ways your students can **show what they've learned** through products, presentations, and conversations.

Table 7-2 shows some examples of end products for young learners.

Table 7-2 End product examples for young learners

Final Product	Description
Class Book	A book created by students that can be shared with families or placed in the school library.
Poster or Artwork	Visual representations of their learning that can be displayed in the community.
Guided Tour or Map	Students create a map or plan a guided tour to teach others about their project topic.
Service Project	A community-focused project, like creating care packages or writing thank-you notes.
Play or Performance	A short play, puppet show, or musical performance that showcases their learning.

You can also incorporate an exhibition event where students present their work to an authentic audience, family, peers, or community members. This not only celebrates their learning but also makes their work feel meaningful and important.

Plan Learning Experiences to Reach Those Goals

Now that you know what you're working toward, you can start planning the activities, lessons, and experiences that will help your students reach those goals.

As students grow plant starts, they record the daily changes they notice.

In the primary classroom, this might include:

- Exploration and play-based learning
- Storytelling and read alouds
- Hands-on projects and art
- Small group or one-on-one guided lessons
- Video clips and short documentaries
- Field trips or virtual expeditions
- Expert visits (in-person or virtual)

When planning, keep your students' developmental levels, interests, and needs in mind. Make sure your lessons are engaging, accessible, and aligned with the learning standards you're focusing on.

You can use a variety of planning and organizing templates found in the Appendix for reproduction or by follow the QR code at the end of this book to plan digitally.

Step 1: Selecting a Topic and End Goal

The first step in planning your PBL unit is selecting a topic that will excite your learners and identifying the end goal you want them to achieve. When working with primary students, you'll want to choose topics that are developmentally appropriate, relevant to their interests, connected to real-world experiences, and that contribute toward their grade level standards. Table 7-3 gives some tips and examples.

To identify the end goal, think about what you want your students to know, understand, and be able to do by the end of the unit. End goals should cover academic goals, social emotional learning goals, speaking and listening goals, and connect to the unit topic.

For example, if writing a unit about recycling in the classroom, consider the following:

- **Academic Goals:** Learn about what harms Earth and different types of materials that can be recycled. Be able to draw and write about recycling to persuade others to join in.
- **Social Emotional Learning Goals:** Students learn how to collaborate by working in small teams to create their end product.
- **Speaking and Listening Goals:** Having group discussions where students listen to the ideas of others, ask questions, and share their ideas.
- **Unit Connection:** Students will hang posters around the school asking others to help them recycle, and place labeled boxes in a common area to collect recycling.

Table 7-3   Selecting a topic and end goal

Consideration	Examples	Tips
Student Interests	Animals, Transportation, Seasons	Ask students or observe what they're curious about.
Real-World Connections	Community Helpers, Recycling	Choose topics that connect to their world.
Developmental Appropriateness	Plants, Weather Patterns	Ensure topics match their cognitive level.
Grade Level Standards	Numbers, Shapes, Alphabet, Letter Writing	Integrate state and national standards.

Your Turn: Using the Unit Brainstorm template, begin to list ideas for topics your students would find engaging, topics that align to your grade level standards, topics that are developmentally appropriate for their age, and finding ways they can connect to academic, Social-Emotional Learning (SEL), and speaking and listening goals you have for your students. Begin to think about types of public products that could potentially come from these unit topic ideas.

Step 2: Planning the Final Product and Presentation

Once you've selected your topic and end goal(s), it's time to outline the details of your unit. This includes thinking about possible activities, lessons, and experiences that will help your students reach those goals. As we backward plan your unit, we will start with planning the final product and the audience and exhibition experience.

Your Turn: Grab your Unit Planning template, and we'll walk through each section as you plan your unit. Remember, none of this is final or set in stone. Everything is fluid and can change as the planning gets fleshed out in the following steps or even as your students begin to work through the unit.

Public Product

The final product is the centerpiece of your PBL unit. It's what your students will create to show what they've learned. The presentation is how they share their product with an authentic audience. When designing a final product for your unit, leave the specific details loose, giving opportunity for students to exercise their voice and choice when making decisions about what they will share during their exhibition event. You will also want to make sure that the product is developmentally appropriate for your student's age and academic level.

A zoo station is set up for guests to tour.

Table 7-4 has some ideas for end products that you could tailor to your student's needs.

Table 7-4 Ideas for end products

Writing Projects	Technology Projects	Math Projects	Community Projects	Creative Projects	Speaking Projects
Letters	Slideshow/ Presentation	Games	Campaigns	Theatrical Performance	Petition
Books	Video Presentation	Surveys	Service Project	Visual Arts (painting, drawing, sculpture)	Tour Guide
Brochure/ Pamphlet	Infographic	Budgets	Public Presentation	Photography	Video Presentation
News Article	Podcast	Maps	Interviews/ Oral Histories	Musical Composition	Panel Q&A
Journal	Commercial	Models	Community Resource Guides	Graphic Novels/ Comics	Digital Storytelling
Blog Post	PSA	Graphs	Teaching Others	Handwork	Audio Recording
Script	Website	Blueprints	Surveys/ Needs Assessment	Community Art Projects	Debate
Poems	Documentary	STEM Integration	Collaborative Art Installation	Posters	Play/ Performance

Authentic Audience

Presenting to an authentic audience makes learning more meaningful by giving students a real-world connection to their work. Planning for an authentic audience involves identifying the right people who will appreciate, learn from, and give feedback on your students' projects. When selecting an authentic audience, consider the project's topic and scope. For example, if your students are creating a class book about animals, their audience could include families, community members, or even local veterinarians.

Planning for your audience means reaching out early, setting expectations, and preparing students to present their work confidently.

As students share their learning, parents have a list of questions they can use to help guide the presentation.

Students could present to:

- Their Families
- Local Community Members
- School Community
- Local Business Owners
- Local Experts
- Their Peers

Exhibition Options

The way students present their work is just as important as the work itself. The exhibition should be an event that showcases their learning journey and final product. Planning an exhibition means thinking through the logistics, including location, format, and audience participation. Exhibitions can be simple or elaborate, depending on the time and resources available. For younger students, consider manageable and meaningful options. For instance, a classroom showcase where students explain their project to visiting families can be just as impactful as a larger school-wide event. Table 7-5 shows more ideas.

Your Turn: Grab your Exhibition Planning template. Once you have selected your exhibition type and you audience, you'll want to also think about how you will contact the audience you want to invite, the location for your event and how to secure it, and materials you'll need for your exhibition. It is good to get this started early in the project unit (or even before you begin) to make sure everything is arranged with your location and any unique audience members needed.

Table 7-5 Exhibition ideas

Exhibition Type	Description
In-Class Showcase	Set up stations for parents to visit.
Virtual Exhibition	Record a video of student presentations.
School-Wide Presentation	School community tours the presentation.
Community Event	Partner with a local community organization or business.
Publishing	Making student work available to the public.
Peer to Peer	Presenting to classmates.
Panel Presentation	Having a selection of community experts to present to.

Step 3: Outline the Unit

Now we will get ready to plan out the actual lessons and activities that take place in each of the modules within the unit. This portion of our planning does take the longest and needs to be the most flexible, but this is where the learning happens! You will incorporate your standards, learning goals and targets, and specific skills students need to master as they move along through the unit.

Planning Lessons and Activities

When brainstorming lessons and activities, think about your project's big concepts and what students need to learn to reach their end goal. Think about the academic standards and developmental goals you established when you selected your final product. Start by outlining these essential skills and knowledge pieces and come up with engaging ways to teach those elements. Lessons should include a mix of hands-on activities, research and reading, art integration, asking and answering questions, discussion, experts and expeditions, and collaborative tasks to meet young learners' developmental needs.

For example, if your students are creating a class poster about how to get ready for lunch, students will need to practice this task, brainstorm steps, photograph or draw the steps, discuss and decide on an order, create the poster, discuss and decide where to hang the poster, implement the poster. Within these steps, they will also want to learn about how-to posters which could include observing other procedural posters, identifying key elements: text size, color, font, imagery, design, layout, etc.

Your Turn: Start to jot down different activities, skills, and lessons your students will need throughout the unit. Do not worry about them being in order. Just write down whatever comes to mind as you think through the end goal/standards and what your students will need to get there. Don't forget to include line items for activities within your unit that work toward the public product, such as days for creating physical materials, writing invitations to the audience, creating posters, etc.

Grouping into Modules

To keep your unit structured and manageable, group your lessons and activities into three sequential modules. Each module should build on the previous one, gradually leading students toward the final product and exhibition. Many of the units outlined in Section 2 follow the below sequence:

- Module 1: Introduction to the Topic
  - Activating schema (prior knowledge)
  - Building background knowledge
  - Research and shared reading
  - Discussions
  - Vocabulary building

- Module 2: Exploring Key Concepts
  - Deepening understanding
  - Hands-on exploration and learning
  - Expeditions
  - Guest speakers
  - Beginning public product elements
  - Group work

- Module 3: Preparing for Public Presentation

  - Applying knowledge and skills
  - Creating or finishing final product
  - Exhibition planning and preparation
  - Invitations
  - Practicing presentations

Within these modules are lessons and activities that spiral and build upon one another toward the end goals and standards. By organizing your unit into modules, you ensure a clear progression that keeps students engaged and focused throughout the project. It also makes planning more manageable, allowing you to focus on one phase at a time.

Your Turn: Grab three colored highlighters and assign them to Modules 1, 2, and 3. Read through your list of lessons and activities you brainstormed and begin to highlight them to identify the module they belong in. Once they have been assigned a module, you will transfer these activities to your PBL Unit Outline. Write down the lessons and activities in a sequential order within each of the three modules.

Check-ins and Assessment

Check-ins and assessments help ensure that students are on track and provide opportunities for feedback and reflection. These can be informal observations, student conferences, or more structured formative assessments. As you teach through a PBL unit, it's not just about getting to the end product and exhibition; it's about the process of getting there and the learning done along the way.

Think about the standards you need your students to master and the developmental goals you have set for them throughout the unit. Look for moments throughout the modules where student work can serve as a check-in point, a formative assessment, or a chance for self-reflection. Look for times when it would be appropriate for a one-to-one conference, team/group conferences, or whole class check-ins. Find ways to tie in self reflection, checking work and collaboration against a checklist or rubric, and planning for making work better.

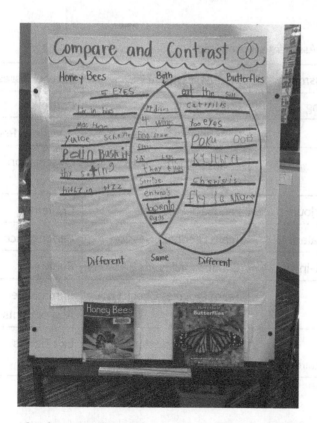

After learning about bees and butterflies, students co-created a Venn Diagram to demonstrate their understanding of the similarities and differences between the insects.

Table 7-6 shows a variety of ways you can assess student learning and standard/goal achievement within PBL units.

Your Turn: Go through your lists of activities within each module and mark moments throughout the module that you can flag as assessment opportunities. Add in specific moments to address assessment, such as adding in a rubric day, a gallery walk, or a more formal skill assessment. Mark elements of the product creation that you will use to assess learning and standards, such as writing samples, math work, or comprehension of their research reading.

Community Involvement: Experts and Expeditions

In a PBL unit, learning gets way more exciting (and impactful) when we bring in **real people** with **real experience** to guide the process.

Table 7-6   Assessment methods

Self-Assessment	Peer Assessment	Teacher Assessment
Goal Setting	Gallery Walk	Portfolios
Check List	Peer Review Rubrics	Anecdotal Records
Rubric	2 Compliments and a Critique	Observation
Reflection Journal	Feedback Protocols	Conferring
Thumb Scale	Team Feedback Session	Performance Tasks
SEL Check-in	Critique Circles	Rubrics
KWL	Team Progress Check List	Summative Assessments
Surveys/ Questionnaires	Fishbowl Discussions	Exit Tickets

A local artist is invited into the classroom to share about their job.

That's where experts and expeditions come in (see Table 7-7). Experts can bring stories, insights, and feedback that make learning feel relevant and real, while expeditions take students out of the classroom to experience their learning firsthand. Together, these elements make PBL more engaging, more authentic, and way more memorable for students.

There are a variety of ways you can include these experts into the PBL unit including:

- **Guest Lectures** (virtual or in-person)
- **Mentorship** throughout the project
- **Panel Discussions** to provide diverse perspectives
- **Feedback and Critiques** on student presentations
- **Hands-On Workshops** to develop skills

Table 7-7   Types of experts and how they can interact with your class

Type of Expert	How They Can Interact with the Class
Scientists and Researchers	Share their latest findings, conduct Q&A sessions, or guide students in conducting experiments.
Industry Professionals	Provide case studies, mentor students in developing projects, and give feedback on presentations.
Local Government Officials	Discuss civic issues, policies, and community challenges to inspire students to take action.
Entrepreneurs and Business Owners	Help students understand problem-solving, budgeting, and innovation processes.
Artists and Designers	Conduct workshops, inspire creativity in projects, and critique student work.
Community Helpers	Provide insights on their careers and how they contribute to the community.
Engineers and Architects	Guide students through design-thinking processes and problem-solving strategies.
Authors and Journalists	Share writing techniques, storytelling tips, and assist students with crafting persuasive arguments.
Environmentalists	Lead field studies, discuss sustainability issues, and help design eco-friendly solutions.
Historians and Cultural Experts	Provide context and stories to deepen students' understanding of historical events.

Expedition Opportunities

When it comes time to plan expeditions, there are myriad opportunities, some of which I list in Table 7-8.

Bringing both experts and expeditions into your PBL units makes learning come alive in a whole new way. It creates a hands-on, real-world experience that gets students thinking, asking questions, and solving problems that actually matter. Plus, it goes beyond just keeping them engaged, it gives them the tools they need to tackle real challenges and make a difference in their communities.

Partner with local outreach and education centers to set up visits connected to your units.

Your Turn: Brainstorm ideas for the types of people and places you can integrate into your unit to deepen student learning and understanding and make the learning more relevant and applicable to their final product. Identify individuals and their contact information, locations and their hours of operation, costs involved, etc. Begin to make these connections and schedule these opportunities before you begin the unit, similar to scheduling the exhibition, to ensure you are not scrambling at the last minute to align these opportunities. If cost is prohibitive, look into classroom parents, grandparents, coworkers, family friends, etc., who may be experts in the field you are researching. Look for expeditions that are low or no-cost, or places that can give discounts for educational purposes.

Table 7-8 Expedition opportunities

Type of Expedition	Purpose and Value
Local Business Tours	Learn about operations, problem-solving, and how the business contributes to the community.
Community Service Projects	Engage in meaningful work that directly impacts the community.
Historical Site Visits	Explore the history and culture of the area, bringing historical concepts to life.
Art Galleries and Museums	Gain inspiration for creative projects and deepen understanding of cultural topics.
Nature Reserves and Parks	Conduct fieldwork, gather data, and explore environmental issues firsthand.
Government Offices or Courtrooms	See civic processes in action and learn about law-making or judicial systems.
Universities or Labs	Observe cutting-edge research and inspire students toward STEM careers.
Cultural Centers	Immerse students in diverse cultures, traditions, and languages within their community and beyond.
Media Outlets	Learn about journalism, storytelling, and media production.
Factories or Workshops	Understand how products are made and explore manufacturing careers.

Students are on a nature walk observing ants in their natural habitat.

Step 4: Design the Driving Question

Creating a strong Driving Question (DQ) is like giving your project a North Star. It keeps your learners (and you!) on course throughout the unit, ensuring that every activity, conversation, and discovery is tied to a meaningful purpose. But crafting a powerful DQ can feel tricky, especially with young children who are still learning to ask their own big questions.

Elements of a Strong Driving Question (DQ)

A Driving Question is not just any question; instead, it's a guiding light that sets the tone for your entire unit. To make sure your DQ hits the mark, it should have three key elements (see Table 7-9).

Table 7-9 Elements of a DQ

Element	What It Means	Example
Open-Ended	The question doesn't have a simple "yes" or "no" answer.	"How can we make our classroom more welcoming for new friends?"
Authentic	It connects to real-world ideas that matter to children.	"How do bees help flowers grow?"
Actionable	It leads to hands-on inquiry and problem-solving.	"How can we build homes for backyard animals?"

TIP When crafting your DQ, ask yourself, "Would my students be excited to explore this?" If it sounds more like a worksheet prompt than a genuine inquiry, keep adjusting!

Question Frames for Young Learners

Sometimes, it helps to use a template or "frame" to get your Driving Question started. Table 7-10 lists some tried-and-true frames that work well in primary PBL units.

Table 7-10 Question frames

Question Frame	Example	Why It Works for Young Learners
How can we. . . .	"How can we take care of our community garden?"	Encourages action and problem-solving.
What happens when. . . .	"What happens when we recycle?"	Promotes curiosity and cause-effect thinking.
Why is. . . important?	"Why is kindness important in our classroom?"	Sparks discussion about values and behavior.
How do. . . work?	"How do fire trucks help people?"	Encourages exploration of systems and roles.

TIP Your project doesn't have to have a set in stone DQ to get started. If you are completely stuck, let your students help shape the question! Try asking them, "What do you wonder about?" or "What do you want to learn more about?" regarding the topic. Their ideas might surprise you and will guide you toward a more meaningful Driving Question.

Your Turn: Grab the template for Developing a Driving Question. First, write the topic you are going to be focusing on for your unit. Next, identify an action word that represents what you want the students to DO within the unit: help, create, build, show, etc. Then select one of the sentence frames above. Insert your action word and topic within the sentence frame. Finally, check if your questions include the three essential elements: open ended, authentic, actionable. (In addition to the DQ for the entire unit, you will notice in the unit plans I provided in Section 2, that I like to have a mini DQ for each of my modules within the unit to help drive the learning and keep it anchored within that module. These are optional, you can also just title your modules or leave them as Module 1, 2, 3.)

Step 5: Planning the Launch

The launch experience should make your students sit up, lean in, and say, "Wow! What are we doing today?" It's a moment of curiosity, surprise, and wonder that invites students into the heart of your PBL unit. The magic of the launch isn't just about the activity itself; it's about how you guide your students to *wonder* and *ask questions*. A great launch doesn't give all the answers; it invites curiosity and opens the door for student-driven inquiry.

Your launch should:

- Present a Problem
- Frame the Project as a Mission
- Give the Project Purpose
- Invite Questions and Wonder
- Offer a Teaser
- Create Anticipation

Table 7-11 lists some sample launch designs to get you started.

 Your Turn: Using a launch idea from above, craft an engaging launch for your unit. Not every launch needs to be big and elaborate. Sometimes, the project topic alone will be exciting to primary students!

Table 7-11 Launch planning

Launch Idea	Example
Mystery Box	Bring in a box with clues related to your project.
Guest Speaker	Invite a community helper or expert to spark inquiry.
Field Trip or Virtual Tour	Explore a local site or do a virtual walk-through.
Big Problem or Challenge	Present a challenge: "Our playground is messy! How can we fix it?"
Letter from a Stakeholder	Asks for assistance solving a problem.
Stations/ Centers	Students rotate through a variety of stations or centers in the classroom to observe, investigate, and begin to wonder.
Video	Showing a problem or from an expert posing a problem that needs solving.
Article	A news article that highlights an issue in the community that students will feel passionately about getting involved in.
Photographs	Observe photographs of elements of the unit topic and/or a problem that needs solving.

Step 6: Setting Up the Project Wall

Think of your **Project Wall** as the classroom's "mission control" for your PBL unit. It's a visual hub that keeps everyone, i.e., students, teachers, and families, on track and engaged. In the primary grades, where young learners thrive on visuals and routines, a well-crafted Project Wall turns abstract concepts into something concrete, dynamic, and interactive.

But here's the key: It's not just a display. A true Project Wall is a **living wall** that evolves alongside your project. It reflects student thinking, celebrates progress, and helps everyone see how their learning connects to the big picture.

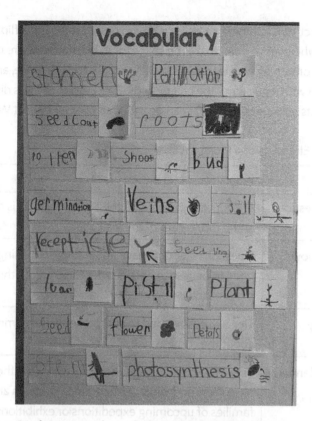

Student created vocabulary is included on the
Project Wall.

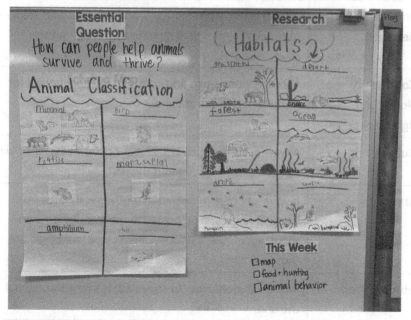

Co-created anchor charts for students to reference are a key part of a
Project Wall.

A Project Wall can be on a bulletin board, dry erase board, a flip chart, on a door, really wherever you can make the space for it. No matter where it is located, it should be something your learners can easily access and reference, and it should be interacted with regularly as the unit unfolds. Every Project Wall is different, but Table 7-12 lists some elements that can be included on your Project Wall.

Table 7-12   Elements of a Project Wall

Element	Why
Driving Question	Anchors the project and the Project Wall. This should be at the top/center of the wall.
Need to Knows	Questions students have about the topic. Things that need to be researched in order to complete the final product and present.
Vocabulary	Tier 3 words needed to comprehend and communicate about the content.
Project Calendar/ Task List	Keeps the class students on track with what they need to have done and when. Also reminds students and families of upcoming expeditions or exhibitions.
Teams	List of who is working together and on what.
Important Resources	Anchor articles, photographs, artifacts, etc., that students may need to reference repeatedly throughout the module or unit.
Community Norms and Agreements	Agreed-upon norms and community expectations for working together throughout the unit.
Rubrics	A way for students to self-assess or know what they will be assessed on throughout the unit.
Standards	If your school administration requires standards or learning targets to be posted in the learning environment, your Project Wall is a great place to incorporate those.
Student Work	Include student work to showcase learning throughout the unit.

Throughout the unit, this wall will grow and change based on the module, learning, inquiry, and student contributions. The Project Wall should not be static and left unchanged but rather be updated regularly with new ideas, new learning, and new work. It isn't a decoration, bulletin board, or poster. It is a tool for discussion, reflection, and reference. Rather than everything on the wall being teacher made, and teacher driven, it should include ample evidence of student ownership and learning.

Sample Project Wall

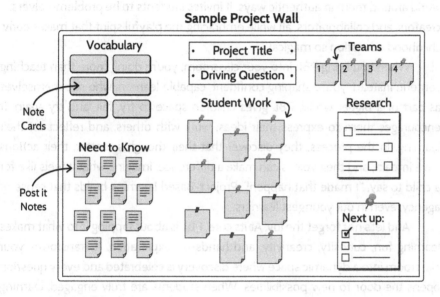

A Project Wall layout sample.

It may look messy but in a good way. The Project Wall will become the anchor in your learning space for your learners and your visitors.

Ready, Set, PBL: The Beginning of the Journey

As we wrap up our journey through Big Projects for Little Learners, take a moment to reflect on what you've just unlocked. Project-Based Learning isn't just a teaching method; it's a mindset shift. It's about empowering young learners to take ownership of their curiosity, ask meaningful questions, and engage with the world around them in authentic ways. It invites students to be problem-solvers, creators, and collaborators, all while embracing the playful spirit that makes early childhood education so magical.

When you bring PBL into your classroom, you're doing more than teaching content; instead, you're shaping confident, capable learners who see themselves as part of a bigger world. PBL gives children space to try, fail, and try again. It encourages them to express their ideas, work with others, and reflect on their learning. In the process, they discover that their thoughts matter, their actions have impact, and their voices can make a difference. Imagine what it feels like for a child to say, "I made that happen!" Project-Based Learning builds that sense of agency, even in our youngest learners.

And let's not forget the joy. At its core, PBL is about tapping into what makes learning fun, curiosity, creativity, and hands-on exploration. It transforms your classroom into a dynamic space where discovery is celebrated and every question opens the door to new possibilities. When students are truly engaged, learning feels like play, and isn't that what early childhood education should be? Project-Based Learning makes learning joyful, meaningful, and memorable, not only for students but also for you as an educator, too.

Yes, planning a PBL unit takes intention and effort. There will be sticky moments and surprises along the way. But isn't that the beauty of learning? When you embrace PBL, you give your students the gift of **real-world learning**, the kind that sticks because it matters. You also give yourself permission to step back and let your students lead. You'll be amazed at the creativity, resilience, and growth that blossom when you trust children to take the reins of their own learning journey.

So, let's do this! Start small, reflect often, and celebrate every success. Whether you're jumping into a unit I wrote just for you, or you are creating your own vibrant project unit, know that you are creating experiences your students will carry with them long after they leave your classroom. PBL is more than a unit plan, it's a way to spark lifelong learning. And that? That's the kind of impact every educator dreams of making.

About the Author

Mikaela Martinez is a passionate educator who believes that learning should be hands-on, meaningful, and full of curiosity. She is the founder of **Project-Based Primary®**, where she creates memberships, curriculum, courses, and teaching resources to support both classroom and homeschool educators. She also owns and teaches kindergarten at **Project-Based Primary School**, a Project-Based Learning (PBL) school for preschool and kindergarten in Coeur d'Alene, ID.

When she's not teaching or writing curriculum, Mikaela loves reading a good book, spending time at the beach, enjoying family movie nights, good snacks, and perusing antique stores with her husband Mario and their daughter. More than anything, Mikaela hopes to inspire other educators to bring joy, creativity, and curiosity into their classrooms every day.

The author (right) with her family

Acknowledgments

Writing this book has been a journey filled with inspiration, support, and encouragement from so many wonderful people. I am deeply grateful for each and every person who has played a role in bringing this book to life.

First and foremost, to my family: my husband Mario and my daughter, thank you for your endless love, patience, and encouragement. Your constant support, whether through late-night writing sessions, encouraging my passion for education, or simply keeping me stocked with good snacks, means more than I can say. Without you both to lean on each day, this book never would have made it out of my brain and onto paper. I love you both so incredibly much.

To the incredible educators, homeschoolers, and members of **Project-Based Primary®**, thank you for your enthusiasm, for cheering me on, and your dedication to making learning meaningful for children. Your passion for teaching and commitment to hands-on, project-based education continually inspire me, and I am honored to be part of your teaching journey.

To the students and families of **Project-Based Primary School**, thank you for allowing me to be part of your learning adventures. Watching young learners explore, question, and grow is truly the heart of everything I do. I cannot wait to see the units in these pages come to life with your children.

To the behind-the-scenes heroes of this book: my editors, proofreaders, designers, and everyone who helped shape these pages at Wiley—thank you for your expertise, patience, and keen eyes. Your work has made this book better in every way. I am so thrilled with how my vision came to life with your dedication and talents! To Sam, I am so grateful you reached out to me and saw something meaningful I could contribute to education.

A huge thank you to the PBP team. To my assistant Sarah who keeps me organized, on task, and on time: Without your spreadsheets, reminders, and skills, Project Based Primary® would be a sinking ship. You keep it afloat, and I am eternally grateful. To Mike, the media man, I am grateful for your keen eye, your dedication to the details, and all the unseen work that you do that makes this journey possible. To Kinsey, for helping to make the materials we share with teachers and families the absolute best they can be! You are the hardest worker I know! Thank you three for your unwavering dedication to the education of young children through the work that you do.

To my friends near and far, thank you for cheering me on, encouraging me when I doubted myself, and reminding me to take breaks when needed (even if I didn't always listen). Your support has meant the world to me. Karissa, my life-long teaching partner, the one always game to try out any unit I wrote, always there to be a listening ear, to support, uplift, and challenge. Thank you times a million.

Finally, to you, the reader: Thank you for being here. Whether you are an educator, a parent, or someone passionate about creating meaningful learning experiences for children, I hope this book brings you inspiration, encouragement, and practical tools to make learning joyful and engaging.

With gratitude,
Mikaela Martinez

Appendix

The planning and organizing templates found in the appendix can be reproduced to guide you in planning your own PBL units. You can also follow the QR code at the end of this book to plan digitally.

Unit Brainstorm Template

Student Interests	Real World Connections	Developmentally Appropriate Topics	Grade Level Standards

Topic Selected:

Academic Goals	Social Emotional Learning Goals	Speaking and Listening Goals	Unit Connection Ideas

Overview Planning Template

Unit Title:	Driving Question:		
Public Product:			
Learning Goals/ Standards:	Length of Unit:		
Potential Expeditions and/or Experts:			
Unit Activity Ideas:			

Exhibition Planning Template

Exhibition Type	
Location	
Materials Needed	
Audience	
Contact Information	

Expert and Expedition Planning Template

Experts	Name and Title	Contact Information	Visit Details

Expeditions	Location	Contact Information	Trip Details

Developing a Driving Question

Topic:	
Action: (What do you want students to DO?)	
Select a sentence frame:	☐ How can we... ☐ What happens when... ☐ Why is... important... ☐ How do ...work...
DQ Question Draft:	
Is your question:	☐ Open ended? Cannot be answered with the words yes or no. ☐ Authentic? Connects to the real world. ☐ Actionable? Leads to problem solving and hands-on inquiry.
Final Driving Question:	
Optional: Module Driving Questions:	Module 1:
	Module 2:
	Module 3:

Project Unit Plans

Title:	
Driving Question:	**Public Product:**
Launch Event:	**Standards & Learning Goals:**

Module 1:
1.

2.

3.

4.

Module 2:
1.

2.

3.

4.

Module 3:
1.

2.

3.

4.

Exhibition:

Experts:	**Expeditions:**
Materials/Supplies:	**Books/Artifacts:**

Online Resources:

Index